Paul Thatcher

Students' Notes on the History of Africa in the 19th and 20th Centuries

LONGMAN

Longman Group Limited
Longman House,
Burnt Mill, Harlow, Essex,
UK.

Associated companies, branches and
representatives in Africa and throughout
the world.

© Longman Group Limited 1981

First published 1981

ISBN 0 582 60362 5

Printed in Singapore by
Huntsmen Offset Printing Pte Ltd

Contents

1

Africa: an introduction

Aims and organisation

During the last twenty years, interest in and understanding of African history has greatly increased. Recent research has done much to destroy earlier myths, correct distortions and add to our knowledge of Africa's varied and exciting past. This book is not a specialist study of any particular aspect of history, but a broad, general introduction to modern African history. Hopefully it will help to serve the needs of both the general reader and the non-specialist student.

Throughout Africa most of the many types of educational institution between junior secondary and university level offer courses in modern African history. Also in other parts of the world a growing number of students are being given the opportunity to study introductory courses in African history. This book has been prepared with the needs of these students very much in mind: it should serve both as a basic framework from which to begin a study of the period and as a revision guide for examination purposes. It has been organised in such a way as to cover those topics most commonly found in modern Africa syllabuses with special emphasis placed on the topics most likely to occur in examination questions.

An attempt is made to deal with the main developments in the history of the different parts of Africa from AD 1800 to the present day. In order to write about such a large subject so briefly, it is necessary to summarise, simplify and select material very carefully. It is, however, important not to simplify to such an extent that the considerable complexity and variety of Africa's past is concealed.

AD 1800 has been chosen as a starting point because most history syllabuses dealing with modern Africa begin from there. The history of the nineteenth century cannot, of course, be understood without some knowledge of earlier events and so some essential background information is given in the first two chapters. Where possible a general theme has been explained with examples drawn from different parts of the continent. Often, however, different regions have had to be treated separately. Any division of Africa into regions is bound to be artificial because all had and have links with each other, but such a division is often necessary. (See Map 1.)

Sources of African history

Students should have some knowledge of the sources of African history, the methods and materials used by historians to find out about the past. The most useful and abundant source for the historian of modern Africa is written records.

1

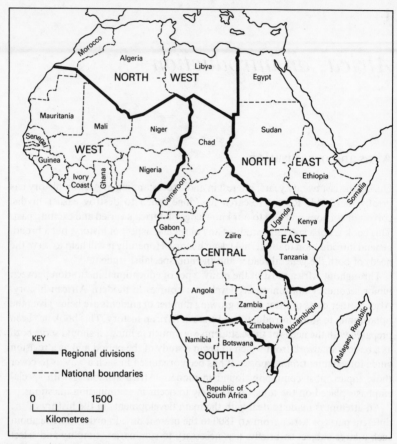

Map 1   Africa: approximate regional divisions

This general category includes a great variety of different types (e.g. letters, newspapers, official documents, treaties and diaries). Generally speaking, more and more written records become available the nearer the present day the period being studied. The availability of written material varies greatly between the different regions of Africa. For most of Africa north of the Sahara desert there is written material (ancient Egyptian, Greek, Roman and later Arab) illustrating the history of the area going back several thousand years. For areas of Islamic penetration (e.g. the Western Sudan and the east coast), some written records in Arabic are available for the last thousand years. For most of the coastal areas of Africa, material written by Europeans is available from the late fifteenth century onwards. However, for the rest of Africa (most of the interior of the continent south of the Sudan and Ethiopia), virtually no written records exist until well into the nineteenth century, and in some cases very little until the establishment of colonial rule at the beginning of the twentieth century. Moreover it should be remembered that many of the written sources have, until recently, been produced by non-African (mostly European) writers. Sources other than written records can therefore be useful even for the modern period.

Archaeology (the study of the material remains of the past) is more essential for the earlier periods of history when no other sources are available. Much, however, can and will be added to our knowledge of nineteenth century Africa when more recent sites are investigated by archaeologists.

An even more important source of information for the nineteenth century is unwritten history, or oral traditions. Many societies had (and still have) a special group whose job was to learn, remember and tell the stories and traditions of their people. The historian must handle oral history very carefully since it depends on human memory which is sometimes unreliable. The collection and study of these unwritten records is only just beginning, but already this type of source material has greatly increased our knowledge of the nineteenth-century history of those large areas of Africa where few written records are available before the twentieth century.

Other sciences can also provide information useful for the historian, for example anthropology, linguistics and botany. For the modern period, however, written records are by far the most important historical source, assisted, where necessary, by oral traditions.

The geography of Africa

History cannot be understood without some knowledge of the geographical environment. Students are strongly advised to refer frequently to a historical atlas to supplement the information given in the maps included in this book.

Africa has an area of over thirty million square kilometres. This makes it the second largest of the continents, more than three times the size of Europe. Naturally such a huge area contains many different types of physical feature, climate, soil and vegetation: the savannah belt and the East African highlands provide a very different environment from the rain forests of the west coast and Central Africa, and the temperate areas of the far south contrast with the tropical lands further north. Africa does not divide easily into geographical regions and it must be remembered when studying the general features of the geography of Africa that the necessary generalisations often conceal a great deal of local variation. The following aspects are among the most important for the historian to bear in mind. (See Maps 2 and 3.)

a) Coast. The coastline of Africa is very regular with no lengthy inlets or peninsulas and few natural harbours, thus greatly limiting the use of the sea as a means of communication.

b) Relief. There are few large areas of lowland. Most of Africa's interior consists of a series of plateaux generally higher in the south and east (between 1,000 and 1,800 m above sea level) than in the north and west (between 300 and 1,000 m above sea level). These plateaux often have steep edges (for example the Drakensberg Mountains of South Africa). Although Africa contains mountain ranges (e.g. the Atlas Mountains) and individual mountains (e.g. Kilimanjaro) of great height, these have not proved to be such important barriers to communication as are mountains in other parts of the world. The Rift Valley system of East Africa stretches for over 6,000 kilometres; it con-

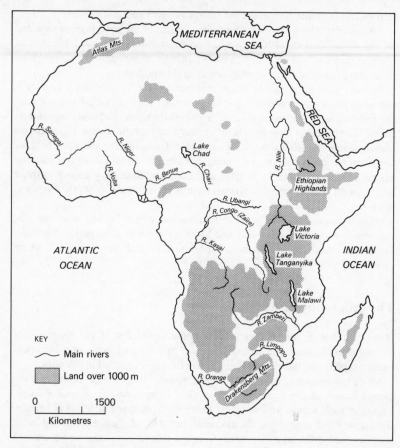

Map 2   Africa: rivers and relief

tains most of the large lakes of East Africa and has fertile soils produced by the volcanoes along its edges.

c) Rivers. The long rivers of Africa have not proved as useful a means of communication as one would have expected. There are many long navigable stretches, but navigation is greatly hampered by numerous rapids and waterfalls (e.g. the Nile cataracts and the waterfalls near the mouth of the Congo).

d) Deserts. The Sahara desert covers much of northern Africa stretching right across the continent from the Atlantic Ocean to the Red Sea, and in south-western Africa there are the less extensive Namib and Kalahari deserts. The Sahara desert has often been regarded as a major barrier seperating the north coast from the rest of the continent, but recent research has tended to stress the role of the Nile valley and trans-Saharan trade routes in the movement of people and ideas. The northern coastal areas are in many ways different from the rest of Africa, but this is more because of their links with the Mediterranean world than because of the Sahara desert.

4

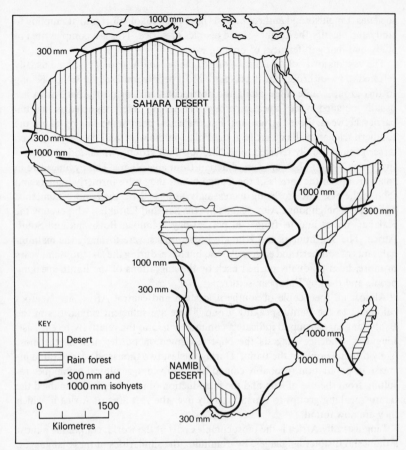

Map 3   Africa: rainfall, forests and deserts

e) Climate. Climatically, rainfall (or rather the lack of it) has been a far more important factor than temperature. In addition to the huge areas of desert where rainfall is virtually non-existant, there are other large areas where rainfall is not sufficient to support much agriculture or a dense population. Even in many of those tropical areas where rainfall is plentiful, agriculture has been handicapped by poor soils produced by leaching, erosion and lateritisation.

f) Disease. The distribution of various diseases has also been of great significance. Especially important is the prevalence in many parts of tropical Africa of the tsetse fly which causes sleeping sickness (trypanosomiasis) and thus severely limits the use of domesticated animals.

The peoples of Africa

Africa contains an enormous variety of peoples, languages, religions, and

5

societies. Linguists and anthropologists have put a lot of effort into attempting to study and classify the languages and peoples of Africa. This is a complex area of study and many differences of opinion exist.

The vast majority of Africans belong to the broad division of mankind usually referred to by anthropologists as Negro. Most people south of the Sahara belong to this group, while those along the north coast and in north-east Africa are usually included in the Caucasian group. The Sahara desert has acted as a partial barrier between these two groups, but there has been some mixing along the southern fringes of the desert (e.g. the Fulani in the west, and, in the east, much larger groups usually referred to as Nilotic). Two groups, which today are relatively small in number, are very different from any others. The pygmies live in small groups in the forests of the Congo basin: they were formerly hunters and food-gatherers, but are being increasingly absorbed by their more numerous agricultural neighbours. Also distinct are the San and Khoikhoi who occupy the Kalahari desert and its fringes in present-day Namibia, Botswana and South Africa. The San hunters and Khoikhoi pastoralists were formerly the main inhabitants of southern and eastern Africa, but have, during the last thousand years or more, been gradually pushed back by the migrations of the Bantu-speaking people and then by European settlers.

Almost all the people of southern, eastern and central Africa are Negroes belonging to the Bantu-speaking group. There are sufficient similarities in the Bantu language group to indicate a common origin in the relatively recent past. Linguistic evidence suggests the Nigeria-Cameroon border area as the most likely original home of the Bantu. During the last two thousand years a rapid increase in population (probably caused by improved agricultural techniques resulting from the use of iron and the introduction of new crops) has enabled the Bantu-speaking groups to expand rapidly over the vast area of Africa in which they are now found.

Linguistically Africa is the most complex part of the world, containing almost a thousand distinct languages. By examining the similarities in these languages, modern scholars have attempted to group them into language families. One such classification has distinguished five main groupings.

a) Niger-Congo (the Bantu languages and most West African languages).
b) Afro-Asiatic (most languages of north and north-east Africa).
c) Macrosudanic (mostly around the upper Nile).
d) Central Saharan (for example Teda and Kanuri).
e) Khoisan (the 'click' languages of the San and Khoikhoi).

Much disagreement still exists about the relationship between different languages and some languages are quite distinct from all their neighbours and do not easily fit into any general classification.

Also very varied is the religious life of the people of Africa. Since the seventh century AD, Islam has spread rapidly to many parts of Africa. Except in Egypt and Ethiopia, Christianity is of much more recent origin. Missionary work during the last century and a half has made Christianity an important element in the religious life of most societies south of the Sahara. The growing popularity of these two great world religions should not, however, lead the student to neglect traditional religion. Anthropological studies (e.g. of the Dinka and Nuer peoples) have shown the complexity and importance of traditional religion.

With such a variety of peoples, languages and religions, it is not surprising that Africa has produced an impressive range of different types of social and political organisation. Many peoples have lived in small egalitarian communities with no formalised political authorities above the local level (e.g. the pastoralist Somali and Maasai, the agricultural Kikuyu and Igbo, and the hunting San). Many others grouped themselves into well-organised states, often large and powerful, with well-developed political institutions (e.g. Buganda, Dahomey and Kano). In between these two extremes can be found societies with varying degrees of political organisation (e.g. the Tuareg confederations, the trading states of the Niger Delta and the small chieftaincies of the Azande and Tswana).

2

Africa to AD 1800

It is not possible to begin the history of Africa abruptly in AD 1800 with no knowledge of earlier developments: the events of the nineteenth century follow on naturally from what had happened earlier. Space permits only the briefest of outlines here. Archaeological discoveries in eastern and southern Africa have produced much evidence to suggest that Africa was the original birthplace of mankind and the scene of most early Stone Age developments. Here, however, we are more concerned with the great themes of the last thousand years: the spread of Islam, the creation of states, the migrations of Bantu-speaking peoples, the increase in trade and the beginning of European contacts. These general themes can best be understood in a regional context.

North-east Africa

This area, dominated by the River Nile, includes the present-day countries of Egypt, Sudan, Ethiopia and Somalia. With the exception of the fertile Ethiopian highlands and the lower Nile valley, most of the area is desert or semi-desert. The extent of our historical knowledge varies greatly: written records and extensive archaeological remains provide detailed information on Egypt for the last five thousand years, whilst, at the other extreme, very little is available on the peoples of southern Sudan until the last hundred years.

The great fertility of the lower Nile facilitated the development in Egypt of one of the greatest civilisations of the ancient world. It was already well-established before 3,000 BC and continued for over 3,000 years. From ancient Egypt agriculture, the domestication of animals and the use of iron spread gradually to other parts of Africa. Especially strongly influenced by Egypt was the middle Nile valley immediately to the south, where the state of Meroë flourished from about 1,000 BC to AD 350.

In 525 BC Egypt was conquered by the Persians: Persian rule was followed by Greek rule and then in 30 BC Egypt became part of the Roman Empire. During the period of Roman rule, Christianity was established in Egypt, where it survives today as the Coptic Christianity of an important minority of Egyptians. From Egypt Christianity spread southwards to the middle Nile area where the kingdoms of Nubia and Alwa were in existence by the sixth century AD. These Christian kingdoms survived until incorporated into the Muslim world between the thirteenth and fifteenth centuries.

On the northern edges of the Ethiopian highlands facing the Red Sea the state of Axum had been created by the third century BC. This area had close connections with southern Arabia and grew strong through trade. The rulers of Axum were converted to Christianity in the fourth century AD and from these origins the Christian empire of Ethiopia developed.

The rapid spread of Arab influence and Islam from the seventh century AD onwards greatly influenced almost the whole of north-east Africa. Egypt was conquered by Muslim Arabs in AD 640 and under successive Muslim dynasties (e.g. the Fatimids and the Ayyubids) gradually adopted Islam, Arab culture and the Arabic language. Under the rule of the Mamluks (1250–1517), Egypt was economically prosperous and militarily strong. After the Ottoman conquest of Egypt in 1517, the Mamluks continued to rule as agents of the Ottoman sultans, but trade declined and Egypt was very weak by the time of the French invasion in 1798.

Most of what now forms the northern half of Sudan was Arabised and Islamised between the fourteenth and eighteenth centuries. The Funj Sultanate of Sennar was founded soon after 1500 and formed the major state of the area. By 1800 the area was strongly Muslim, but the Funj Sultanate had declined and no powerful states existed. Arabic influence and Islam did not spread further south, and little is known of the history of the peoples of southern Sudan (e.g. the Shilluk and Dinka) before 1800.

From the twelfth century onwards the Ethiopian state, centred on the highlands, grew in strength. Here Christianity survived despite serious Muslim threats, e.g. the attacks by the Somali leader, Mohammed Gran in the sixteenth century. Also in the sixteenth century Ethiopia was much weakened by the influx of large numbers of Galla pastoralists. By 1800 the Ethiopian emperor at Gondar had little power and the rivalries between the virtually independent war-lords ruling the main provinces greatly weakened the country.

From a very early date Arab traders and Islam were established at ports around the Horn of Africa (e.g. Zeila and Mogadishu). Islam spread rapidly among the Somali and Danakil people and further inland began to influence the Galla and Sidama. By 1800 Somali pastoralists controlled most of the Horn area, while on the southern fringes of the Ethiopian highlands small Galla and Sidama states (e.g. Kaffa) were thriving.

North-west Africa

This is the area occupied by the present-day countries of Morocco, Algeria, Tunisia and Libya. The northern part between the Sahara desert and the Mediterranean sea is often referred to as the Maghrib (the Arabic for 'West'). Three main geographical divisions can be distinguished: the narrow coastal plain, the Atlas Mountains and the huge desert interior. Most states which have developed in the area have based their power on the coastal areas and have exercised little control over the mountains, let alone the desert. The majority of the inhabitants belong to the Berber group which has survived the frequent influx of foreign settlers.

From about 800 BC the coastal areas were dominated by Phoenicians who founded the great trading city of Carthage. In the third century BC a long conflict began between Carthage and Rome at the end of which Carthage was conquered and most of the Berber states near the coast were incorporated into the Roman Empire. Under Roman rule the coastal area flourished, Christianity was introduced and there was considerable urbanisation and prosperity, but Roman rule was not extended to the interior. The collapse of Roman rule in the fourth century AD was followed by conquests by the Vandals, then by the Byzantines and finally at the end of the seventh century AD by the Arabs. By the end of the eighth century most of the Maghrib had accepted Islam, and Muslim Arab dynasties had been established centred on such important new cities as Kairouan and Fez.

Little is known about the early history of the Sahara, although the discovery of rock-drawings of chariots suggests that long-distance trade across the desert was established at a very early date. Communication in the Sahara was made much easier by the widespread use of the camel from about AD 400 onwards, and soon after this several trade routes were in regular use linking the Maghrib with the Western Sudan. The few inhabitants the desert supported were mainly nomadic Berber groups such as the Zenata, Sanhaja and Tuareg.

During the eleventh century large groups of nomadic Arabs (especially the Banu Hilal and the Banu Sulaim) moved into the Maghrib causing considerable destruction. Between the eleventh and thirteenth centuries most of the Maghrib was united under successive Berber Empires (the Almoravid and then the Almohad Empire). These large empires were followed by smaller, Berber-ruled states (for example the Hafsid state of Tunisia). Frequent Spanish and Portuguese attacks on the north coast in the late fifteenth and sixteenth centuries led to important changes. In Morocco the European threat was crushed by a powerful new dynasty, the Saadians, one of the greatest of whom, Mulay al-Mansur, invaded Songhai at the end of the sixteenth century. The rest of the Maghrib developed into three generally unstable and virtually independent provinces of the Ottoman empire: Algiera, Tunis and Tripoli.

By 1800 much of north-west Africa was in a state of weakness and confusion. Morocco, ruled by the Alawite sultans, had declined greatly and was unable to control most of the Berbers of the mountains. Of the three Ottoman provinces, Tunis under its Husainid beys was the most stable and prosperous, while the Ottoman governors of Algiers and Tripoli had virtually no control over the interior. In the mountains most of the Berbers lived in small, independent village-states, while loosely-organised Berber confederacies controlled the desert and its important trade routes.

West Africa

West Africa is the area bounded on the south and west by the Atlantic Ocean, on the north by the Sahara desert and on the east by the Cameroon Mountains and the low-lying area around Lake Chad. Most of it consists of the open savannah lands of the Western Sudan while along the coast there is a narrow belt of tropical forest. The area includes several large rivers (e.g. the Niger, Senegal and Volta) and the absence of natural barriers has greatly facilitated communications and the growth of large states. Most of the peoples of West Africa are Negroes, mixed in the northern part with Caucasians originally from further north and east. Little archaeological work has yet been done, but already excavations in the central area of Nigeria have shown the existence of the well-developed Nok culture as early as 500 BC.

The Arabic writers of the tenth and eleventh centuries (e.g. Al-Bakri) provide us with the earliest written records for West Africa. They tell of an already flourishing trade between the Western Sudan and North Africa (based largely on the export of West African gold) and the existence of several large states in the Western Sudan (e.g. Ghana and Kanem). For over a thousand years the Western Sudan was dominated by a series of large trading empires: Ghana, until greatly weakened by the Almoravids in the eleventh century; Mali, from the thirteenth to the fifteenth century; and Songhai, in the late fifteenth and sixteenth centuries. Further east several Hausa city-states developed, while the Lake Chad area was controlled by the Kanem-Borno empire ruled from the ninth century onwards by the Sefawa dynasty. To all these states the trans-Saharan trade was vital, and through trading links with North Africa Islam spread gradually to become the dominant religion of the rulers and traders. The trading cities of the Western Sudan (e.g. Timbuktu and Jenne) became centres of Islamic scholarship, but the majority outside the cities were not converted to Islam until the nineteenth century. The Moroccan invasion of Songhai in 1591 led to the collapse of the empire and its replacement by smaller states. Another important development in the 500 years before 1800 was the gradual dispersal of the Fulani right across the Western Sudan from their original homeland in the Senegal area. A complex mixture of peoples lived in the more southern savannah lands, some forming states (e.g. the Mossi-Dagomba states) while others lived in segmentary societies (e.g. the Senufo and Tiv).

Less is known about the early history of the peoples of the coastal area. The terracotta and bronze sculptures of Ife and Benin indicate thriving civilisations in this area long before the beginnings of European contact in the fifteenth century. From the late fifteenth century onwards, the Portuguese and then other European powers, especially the British and French, began trading with the coastal peoples. This trade soon became largely concerned with transporting slaves to the new European colonies in the Americas: between the sixteenth and nineteenth centuries at least fifteen million people were taken from Africa as slaves. This period also witnessed the consolidation of many coastal states such as the Wolof state, Asante (the last and greatest of numerous Akan states), Dahomey, the Oyo Empire and Benin. In other parts of the coastal area less large-scale political units developed, for example the trading cities of the Niger Delta.

Throughout West Africa by 1800 there were signs of important changes soon to come. During the eighteenth century Fulani-led jihads (holy wars) succeeded in creating Muslim states in Futa Jallon and Futa Toro. This provided inspiration and encouragement to the small groups of devout Muslims (often Fulani) in other parts of the Western Sudan who were dissatisfied with oppressive, non-Islamic government. In the west the strongest states were the Bambara states of Segu and Kaarta, while a much-weakened Borno Empire and the prosperous Hausa states (e.g. Kano and Gobir) dominated further east. In the coastal area the foundation of Sierra Leone in 1787 as a home for freed slaves symbolised the growth, especially in Britain, of a humanitarian movement to abolish the slave trade. This helped to produce an increased European interest in West

11

Africa in the form of exploration, Christian missionary work, and attempts to replace the slave trade by trade in other items. In 1800 some coastal states (e.g. Oyo and Benin) were weaker than before, while others (e.g. Dahomey and Asante) were at the height of their power.

Central Africa

Central Africa is here used to refer to the huge central core of the continent stretching from the Sahara in the north to the Limpopo valley in the south, and from the Cameroon Mountains and the Atlantic in the west to the Great Lakes in the east. It includes high plateaux, large rivers (especially the Congo and its tributaries), dense forests and open savannah lands. The majority of the population are Negroes speaking Bantu languages.

The most important development during the last 2,000 years has been the gradual expansion of the Bantu-speaking people thoughout the area. It appears likely that Bantu-speaking groups moved from an original home in the upper Benue valley to the southern areas of present-day Zaïre. From there a rapidly growing population produced migrations in all directions beginning about 2,000 years ago and continuing until the nineteenth century. This great movement of the Bantu-speaking groups affected the whole area and much of East and South Africa as well.

Central Africa north of the River Congo (Zaïre) is an area of low density of population. This, coupled with the relative lack of valuable raw materials and consequent late development of long-distance trade, led to little early state formation. In the far north the states of Wadai and Bagirmi, linked with the Muslim trading system of northern Africa, developed in the sixteenth century. Elsewhere the people lived in small chieftaincies, such as those of the Mbum and Tikar in the Cameroon highlands and the Azande of the Nile-Congo watershed, or they were grouped in small village communities such as those of the Fang and Mongo.

During the centuries before 1800 Central Africa south of the Zaïre forests was influenced by three main factors: the spread of state formation, contact with the Portuguese and the growth of long-distance trade. In the area of Zambia and southern Zaïre, the Luba state and the two main Lunda states (Mwato Yamvo and Kazembe) had become large and powerful by 1800. The once-powerful states of Kongo and Ndongo south of the mouth of the Congo had disintegrated before 1800. Much of present-day Angola was disrupted in the late sixteenth century by groups of warriors known as the Jaga and Imbangala who eventually formed the trading states of Ovimbundu and Kasanje in eastern Angola. Further east, between the rivers Zambezi and Limpopo, gold deposits assisted the early development of states, firstly the Mwene Mutapa Empire and then the Rozwi confederacy. In the central Angola and lower Zambezi areas the Portuguese were active from the sixteenth century onwards in trade in slaves and gold. By 1800 the Portuguese settlements were weak and exerted little control away from the coast. The peoples of the interior were linked to both the west and east coast by several trade routes controlled in the west by such groups as the Imbangala and Ovimbundu and in the east by the Bisa, Bemba and Yao.

East Africa

The coast of East Africa (the present-day countries of Kenya, Uganda and Tanzania) has had trading contacts with other parts of the world for at least the last 2,000 years. By AD 1000 there were prosperous trading cities (e.g. Kilwa and Sofala) containing Arab traders who brought Islam with them. Contact between African and Arab produced the distinctive Swahili language and culture. After a brief period of Portuguese rule, many of the coastal cities again began to fall under Omani Arab influence during the eighteenth century.

The pre-1800 history of the interior is complicated by migrations into this area of many peoples from the north (Nilotic people) and from the west (Bantu-speaking people). Only near the fertile northern and western shores of Lake Victoria did centralised states develop, such as Bunyoro-Kitara, Nkore, Rwanda and Buganda (which was the most powerful by 1800). Most of the other peoples of the interior (e.g. the Hehe, Sukuma, Kikuyu and Luo) lived in small chieftaincies or in village communities.

By the beginning of the nineteenth century the growth of trade (especially in slaves and ivory) between the interior and the coast was starting to influence some of these peoples, especially the Nyamwezi.

Southern Africa

This can be defined approximately as the area covered by the present-day countries of South Africa, Namibia, Lesotho, Swaziland and Botswana. Most of the interior consists of high plains (the veld) with the very high Drakensberg Mountains seperating these interior plateaux from the eastern coastal plain. The crucial geographical factor is rain, which is plentiful on the east coast but decreases westwards until becoming virtually non-existant in the Namib desert of the west coast.

A thousand years ago the thinly-scattered population was made up entirely of San hunters and Khoikhoi pastoralists, but today these two groups are found only in and around the Kalahari desert of the west. During the five hundred years before 1800 these peoples had been gradually pushed out of the more fertile areas by Bantu-speaking groups, in the most southerly extension of the Bantu migrations. By 1800 several distinct groups of southern Bantu can be distinguished.

a) The Nguni (sub-divided into many groups such as the Xhosa, Thembu, and Zulu), still expanding southwards down the eastern coastal plain.

b) The Sotho, occupying most of the interior plains.

c) The Venda in the northern mountains.

d) The Thonga along the north-east coast.

e) The Herero and Ambo in the far west.

These peoples lived in hundreds of small chieftaincies rather than in large states, but already in 1800 the first signs of revolutionary changes among the northern Nguni were beginning to appear.

Southern Africa was the only part of the continent in 1800 to contain large numbers of European settlers. The Dutch had first settled at the Cape in 1652 and their settler-farmer community expanded gradually, the Dutch reaching the Orange River in 1760 and the Great Fish River in 1779. These settlers, known as the Boers, developed a distinctive language (Afrikaans) and an isolated, independent way of life. From the beginning they were racially prejudiced and as they came into greater conflict with the Africans, whose land they stole, they became even more convinced of their own racial superiority. In 1779 they fought the first of many wars against the still-expanding Nguni on the Great Fish River (the first Xhosa war). A large population of people of mixed blood (known as Coloureds) developed and many of these (e.g. the Griqua and Korana) moved into the interior at the end of the eighteenth century. The British conquered the Cape from the Dutch first in 1795 and finally in 1806.

3

North-east Africa in the nineteenth century

The most important aspects of this topic are the development of Egypt with special reference to the work of Mehemet Ali and Khedive Ismail, the Mahdiyya movement in the Sudan, and the reunification and expansion of Ethiopia especially the achievements of Emperor Menelik II.

Egypt under Mehemet Ali

His rise to power

The invasion of Egypt by the French, led by Napoleon in 1798, provides a good starting point for the history of modern Egypt. At the Battle of the Pyramids the French easily defeated the Mamluks (originally ex-slaves of foreign origin) who for centuries had ruled Egypt as part of the Ottoman (Turkish) empire. Disease, British hostility and changes in France caused a rapid French withdrawal, completed by 1801.

Egypt was left in chaos with three groups struggling to assert control: the Mamluks, the Ottoman representatives, and Mehemet Ali, an ambitious Albanian originally sent to Egypt by the Ottoman authorities. Using a skilled mixture of diplomacy and force, Mehemet Ali soon took control and in 1806 was recognised by the Ottoman sultan as 'wali' (governor) of Egypt. He destroyed the last remnants of Mamluk power in 1811 and from then until his death in 1849 he was the leading figure in the history of north-east Africa and the founder of the modern Egyptian state.

Internal achievements

Mehemet Ali's main aim was to establish the hereditary rule of his family free from Ottoman control. To achieve this Egypt had to be made strong and so he embarked on a wide range of modernising reforms, making use of European, especially French, experts and skills wherever necessary.

a) Military reforms. The army was greatly expanded and provided with the most up-to-date training and weapons, and a large navy was created.

b) Educational reforms. Foreign experts were recruited and Egyptian students were sent abroad for higher education. Priority was given to science, and schools of medicine, engineering and translation were established.

c) Agricultural reforms. Improved irrigation (including the building of many canals) brought new areas under cultivation and enabled two or three crops to be grown a year instead of one. Subsistence farming was replaced by a cash-crop economy with high quality cotton soon becoming Egypt's main export and chief source of government revenue. The creation of a system of state monopolies prevented the ordinary peasant-farmers from gaining much from these reforms.

d) Industrial reforms. Iron and steel, shipbuilding and textile industries were established, but intense European competition prevented any lasting success.

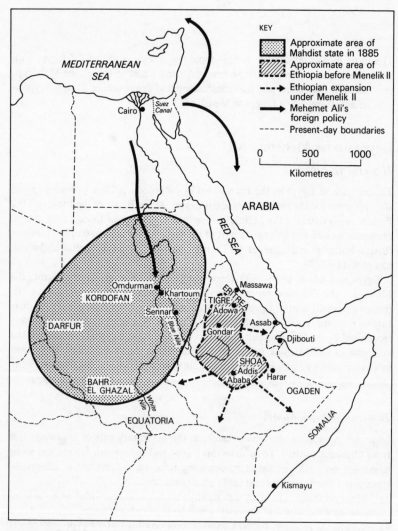

Map 4   North-east Africa in the nineteenth century

Foreign policy

Just as important were Mehemet Ali's achievements outside Egypt.

a) Red Sea area. Between 1812 and 1818 the armies of Mehemet Ali crushed the Wahhabi movement in Arabia and restored western Arabia to Ottoman control. This led to a great revival of trade around the Red Sea affecting the whole area, including Ethiopia. The acquisition of the Red Sea ports of Suakin and Massawa in 1846 further increased Egyptian interest and influence in the area.

b) Sudan. In 1820–21 an army led by Mehemet Ali's son Ismail conquered much of Sudan including the decaying Funj Sultanate of Sennar. Egyptian control of Sudan was caused by a desire for gold, slaves and army recruits and continued until the Mahdiyya movement of the 1880s.

c) Europe. During the 1820s Egyptian assistance was given to the Ottoman sultan in his struggle against Greek nationalism. Twice during the 1830s Mehemet Ali fought the Ottoman Empire, but on both occasions the great powers of Europe intervened to preserve the empire. In 1841 European pressure forced Mehemet Ali to sign the Treaty of London by which his territorial ambitions in the Middle East and the size of his army were limited in return for recognition of his family's right to rule Egypt as a self-governing province of the Ottoman empire.

Egypt after Mehemet Ali

Egypt stagnated under Mehemet Ali's less able successor, Abbas I (1849–54), and during the reign of Said (1854–63), the most important development was the beginning of the building of the Suez Canal in 1859. It was not until the reign of Khedive Ismail (1863–79) that the work of Mehemet Ali was continued. During his reign Egypt was modernised very rapidly: over 1,500 kilometres of railway were built, the Suez Canal was completed (1869), and education and agriculture were improved. But no attempt was made to industrialise. During the 1870s Ismail attempted to extend Egyptian control even further into the heart of Africa. Much more of Sudan was conquered, Egyptian control was extended up the Nile as far as present-day Uganda, Ethiopia was unsuccessfully attacked and many east coast ports (e.g. Zeila and Kismayu) were temporarily occupied.

These impressive projects at home and abroad were expensive and Ismail appears to have had little financial understanding. He borrowed more and more from European bankers often at exorbitant rates of interest. By 1878 Egypt was bankrupt and Ismail was forced to accept a joint Anglo-French control of Egyptian finances. Dissatisfaction with Ismail's government and the growth of European intervention produced a nationalist movement led by army officers such as Urabi Pasha. In 1879 Ismail was deposed, and under his son and successor Tewfiq, European control of Egyptian affairs increased leading to a nationalist uprising in 1881. But the British invaded Egypt in 1882, defeated the nationalists and established a British-controlled government, the first step in the partition of Africa. In theory the khedive and his ministers continued to rule Egypt, but in practice real power was in the hands of the British Consul-General, a position held by Lord Cromer from 1883 to 1907.

Sudan in the nineteenth century

Turco-Egyptian Rule 1820–81

The central and northern areas of the present-day Sudan Republic were conquered by the Egyptians in 1820–21. Egyptian control was extended towards the
Red Sea and the Ethiopian highlands later in Mehemet Ali's reign, and under
Ismail in the 1870s Egyptian rule was spread westwards to Darfur and southwards
to the Bahr el Ghazal and Equatorial regions. This huge area was divided into
provinces all under the control of a Governor-General with his capital at Khartoum at the junction of the White and Blue Niles. Egyptian rule can be criticised
because of oppressive taxation and corruption, but it did produce some benefits.
Improvements were made in communications, trade and agriculture, and the
diverse peoples of this large area were for the first time provided with some form
of political unity.

The marshes of the Sudd and the opposition of the Shilluk people delayed
Egyptian expansion further south until the 1840s. Egyptian administration was
never firmly established in southern Sudan, but traders seeking slaves and ivory
devastated large areas (e.g. during the 1860s Zubair Pasha with a thousand armed
followers was capturing about 2,000 slaves a year in the Bahr el Ghazal). By the
1870s an increasing number of Christian Europeans were being employed in the
administration of Sudan (e.g. Gordon was made Governor-General in 1877) and
some attempt was being made to suppress the slave trade.

The Mahdiyya 1881–98

In 1881 Mohammed Ahmad, a pious Muslim teacher, declared himself the
Mahdi, a divine leader chosen by God to bring justice to the world. Several
factors help to explain the rise and success of the Mahdiyya movement.
a) A desire to reform and purify Islam.
b) Dissatisfaction with oppressive Egyptian rule.
c) Opposition to the appointment of Christians.
d) Opposition to attempts to end the profitable slave trade.
e) The collapse of the authority of the Khedive in Egypt.

Drawing his military strength largely from the nomadic Baqqara people of
Kordofan, the Mahdi captured El Obeid, the capital of Kordofan, in 1883 and in
1885 entered Khartoum, where General Gordon, sent by the British to evacuate
the Egyptian forces, was killed.

By the time of the Mahdi's death later in 1885, Egyptian forces remained in
control only of the port of Suakin and the Equatoria region. From 1885 the
Mahdist state was ruled by the Baqqara leader, Khalifa Abdullahi, from his
capital at Omdurman. Although much of the earlier religious fervour was lost,
Abdullahi succeeded in crushing rivals, preserving unity, restoring order and
developing an effective, centralised, Islamic administration. By the 1890s the
partition of Africa was well under way and the Mahdist state was threatened on
all sides: by Italians in Eritrea, by Ethiopia, by the French in the west, the Belgians in the south-west, and the British and Egyprians in the north. In 1898 a
large Anglo-Egyptian army defeated Abdullahi at the bloody battle of Omdurman and Sudan fell under Anglo-Egyptian control.

Nineteenth-century Ethiopia

Ethiopia in the early nineteenth century

During the first half of the nineteenth century Ethiopia was a weak, isolated and divided nation. Real power was in the hands of the constantly warring governors ('rases') of the main provinces (e.g. Tigre, Wallo and Shoa) rather than in the hands of the puppet emperors at Gondar. The general confusion and insecurity was increased by the continuing migrations of Galla onto the southern highlands. There were, however, some hopeful signs: Christianity continued to be a unifying force for the peoples of the highlands and memories of a glorious imperial past survived. By the middle of the century trade with the Red Sea area was beginning to revive and the expansion of Egyptian authority southwards and the establishment of European consulates at Massawa was beginning to end Ethiopia's isolation. In the second half of the century, Ethiopia's position was completely transformed by three remarkable emperors.

Tewodros II (1855–68) and Yohannis IV (1871–89)

Tewodros II began the creation of modern Ethiopia. The following were among his achievements.
a) An increase in the authority of the emperor and a weakening of the independent power of the rases.
b) The creation of a large army, equipped with modern weapons.
c) Greater centralisation of the administration and an improved system of taxation.
d) The establishment of diplomatic relations with foreign states.

In many ways Tewodros attempted to reform too rapidly for by the mid-1860s he was generally unpopular. A minor diplomatic incident led to a British invasion in 1868 and, with few supporters left, Tewodros was defeated at Magdala and committed suicide.

The British immediately withdrew and, after a period of unrest, Yohannis IV became emperor in 1871. He consolidated much of Tewodros's internal work, but most of his reign was spent in resisting external threats.
a) During the early 1870s Egypt occupied the major ports along the coast of the Red Sea and most of Eritrea. Except for the conquest of Harar in 1875, Egyptian invasions of the Ethiopian highlands were decisively defeated. Egyptian expansion had ended by the 1880s and Egypt withdrew from all her conquests except a few Red Sea ports.
b) The next threat came from the Italians, who in 1882 seized the Red Sea ports of Assab and Massawa and much of the Eritrean coast. In 1887 the Italians invaded Ethiopia, but were defeated at the battle of Dogali.
c) Another threat came from the newly-established Mahdist state to the north-west. In fact, Yohannis was killed at the battle of Metemma in 1889, as his forces were defeating the Mahdist army.

Throughout Yohannis's reign, Menelik, the ras of Shoa greatly extended his power by acquiring large quantities of guns from the Italians (who wrongly thought Menelik would act as their ally against Yohannis). So powerful was

19

Menelik that Yohannis was forced to accept him as his successor, and so in 1889 the ras of Shoa became emperor as Menelik II.

Menelik II (1889–1913)

Menelik II continued the work of reuniting, expanding and modernising Ethiopia. Even before becoming emperor, Menelik had built up a strong army equipped with modern guns and had extended Ethiopian control to the east and south (e.g. Harar was captured in 1887).

As emperor, Menelik's greatest achievement was the preservation of Ethiopia's full independence. The partition of Africa by the European powers was at its height during the early years of Menelik's reign, and the main threat to Ethiopia came from Italy, already well-established in Eritrea to the north and Somalia to the south-east. The 1889 Treaty of Ucciali, intended by Menelik purely as a treaty of friendship, was used by the Italians to claim that Ethiopia was an Italian protectorate. Such claims were totally rejected by Menelik and preparations for war began. The Italians invaded in 1895 and, after some initial successes, were completely defeated at the battle of Adowa in 1896. Over 7,000 Italians were killed, making Adowa the most decisive European defeat during the partition. By the 1896 Treaty of Addis Ababa, the Italians recognised Ethiopia's independence, which was preserved for the rest of Menelik's long reign by skilful diplomacy.

Menelik also more than doubled the size of his empire, extending Ethiopian control far off the highlands; e.g. the Ogaden, Bale and Sidamo areas were conquered in 1891, and in 1898 his conquests reached as far south as Lake Turkana.

Moreover, Menelik provided Ethiopia with the foundations of a modern state.
a) Addis Ababa was created as a new capital.
b) Currency and a postal service were introduced.
c) Much was done to improve communications. (The Djibouti to Addis Ababa railway was completed soon after Menelik's death in 1917.)
d) Modern education, banking and health services were begun.

Thus Ethiopia entered the twentieth century as a strong, independent nation surrounded on all sides by the colonial acquisitions of the European powers.

4

North-west Africa in the nineteenth century

The most important aspects of this topic are the growth of European influence (especially the French conquest of Algeria), Berber resistence to the French led by Abdel Kader, and the Senussiya movement.

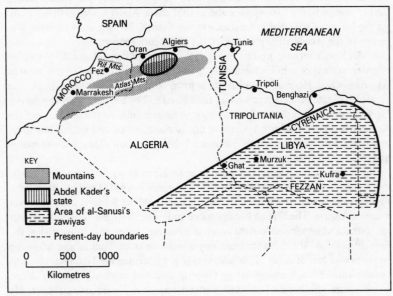

Map 5   North-west Africa in the nineteenth century

Nineteenth-century Algeria

Early nineteenth century

In the early nineteenth century Algeria was nominally part of the decaying Ottoman (Turkish) empire, but in practise the Turkish governor (known as the 'Dey') was virtually independent. The Dey effectively ruled only the cities of the coastal strip (e.g. Algiers, Oran and Constantine), no attempt being made to control the many Berber groups of the interior. In the first decades of the century, the Dey's government was on good terms with France and trade between the two countries flourished. During the 1820s, however, this good relationship broke down as a result of several minor incidents, mostly connected with the activities of the

21

French Consul Deval. The French king, Charles X, hoped (mistakenly as it proved) that a victory overseas would restore his popularity at home, and so in 1830 the French conquered Algiers and the other main Algerian ports and overthrew the Dey's government. This French invasion was the first step in the creation of a huge French empire in North Africa and marked a turning-point in the history of the area.

Abdel Kader

The French conquered the main coastal cities quite easily, but in order to be secure they had to extend their authority to the neighbouring areas. This proved very difficult since the strongly Muslim Berber population valued their independence dearly and regarded the French not only as foreign conquerors but also as Christian infidels threatening their religion. Many previously hostile Berber groups began to cooperate and in 1832 chose Abdel Kader as their sultan. As the leader of nationalist resistance to the French, he soon showed himself to be one of the ablest African leaders of the nineteenth century.

Abdel Kader rapidly brought a large area under his control and developed an effective system of administration, thus laying the foundations of the modern Algerian state. He made Tekedemt, a town south of Oran, his capital, and divided his state into eight provinces each governed by a close friend or relative. He was a devout Muslim and based his government fully on the teachings of the Koran using purely Islamic systems of taxation, education and justice. His statebuilding achievements are especially remarkable since most of his time and energy had to be spent fighting the French.

For fifteen years Abdel Kader led a courageous guerrilla campaign against increasingly large French armies. In 1834 and again in 1837 (Treaty of Tafna) the French were forced to make peace and recognise Abdel Kader's authority over much of Algeria. The French became more and more determined to crush Berber resistance and continued to fight cruel, destructive campaigns. In the 1840s, the French isolated Abdel Kader from any assistance from Tunisia and Morocco and deprived him of many of his followers (e.g. by turning the Tijaniyya Muslims against him). French armies led by General Bugeaud gradually conquered one district after another and in 1847 Abdel Kader was forced to surrender. He spent the rest of his long life in exile.

The completion of French conquest

To retain control of the coastal areas the French had to keep large armies in Algeria and rebellions (e.g. in the Kabylia Mountains in the 1870s) were frequent. Many parts of the Atlas Mountains were not brought completely under French rule until the end of the nineteenth century, and the desert areas retained their independence even longer.

The Berbers were deprived of most of the best land in the coastal plains to make room for French settlers. By the middle of the century there were about 100,000 European settlers in Algeria and by 1900 about half a million. The settlers, some farming large estates but most living in the growing cities, kept in close contact with France and were of slight benefit to the development of Algeria. In the coastal area some attempt was made to introduce French law and culture – with limited success – while most of the interior was ruled indirectly.

Nineteenth-century Morocco

Throughout the nineteenth century Morocco was ruled by sultans of the Alawite dynasty, the most important of whom were Moulay Suleiman (1792–1822), Abdel Rahman (1822–59) and Moulay Hassan (1873–94). These rulers succeeded in preserving Morocco's independence despite increasing European interest, and struggled to extend the area under effective government control (known as the 'bilad al-makhzan') into the Atlas and Rif Mountains and the fringes of the Sahara.

Most of Moulay Suleiman's reign was spent in suppressing a series of rebellions. Abdel Rahman was much involved in the lengthy war in neighbouring Algeria between the Berbers led by Abdel Kader and the French. At first Abdel Rahman used the conflict to extend Moroccan control into western Algeria, but the strength of Muslim feeling soon produced Moroccan support for Abdel Kader. This continued until the French attacked Morocco and defeated its army at the battle of Isly in 1845. Moroccan weakness was further displayed by its defeat by Spain in a war in 1859–60 which increased the area on the north coast ruled by Spain. By this time European activity inside Morocco had greatly increased, the British becoming very involved in the trade of Morocco.

Morocco was strengthened during the reign of the greatest nineteenth-century sultan, Moulay Hassan. He began to develop a modern army and greatly extended the area under Moroccan control. Through skilful diplomacy, he preserved Morocco's independence during the opening years of the partition, making full use of rivalries between the European powers, and especially of the rivalry between the British and the French. Less successful was Abdel Aziz who became sultan in 1894. He was strongly influenced by European advisers and soon owed large sums of money to European bankers. From 1907 onwards the French began to occupy Morocco, most of which was officially declared a French protectorate in 1912. The Spanish gained the north coast.

Nineteenth-century Tunisia

At the beginning of the nineteenth century Tunisia was nominally a province of the Ottoman Empire, but for a century the Husainid dynasty (of Turkish origin) had provided rulers (known as 'Beys'), who were virtually independent of Ottoman authority. Without mountain or desert barriers to contend with, the Beys of Tunis ruled over a more prosperous, better-organised state than their neighbours in Algiers and Tripoli. European interest in Tunisia increased throughout the century, but rivalries between the European powers helped the Beys to retain independence until 1881.

One of the ablest Tunisian rulers during the nineteenth century was Ahmed Bey (1835–55). He laid the foundations of a modern army, navy and education system, using French experts where necessary. In the early 1840s he abolished the trans-Saharan slave trade, the first North African ruler to do so.

The next Bey, Mohammed es Sadek, was less successful. He continued many of Ahmed's modernising reforms, but, like Khedive Ismail of Egypt, his lack of financial good sense led to increasing debts to European bankers. In 1861 a European-style constitution was introduced providing for a representative assembly and for complete legal equality. The failure to implement these constitutional reforms fully led later to the formation of the 'Destour' (meaning constitution) party. By 1869 Tunisia was almost bankrupt and the Bey was forced to accept European supervision of his finances.

During the 1870s the French were determined to add Tunisia to their North African empire and were delayed only because of British and Italian opposition. In 1881 the French invaded and forced the Bey to agree to the Treaty of Bardo, and in 1883 to the Treaty of Marsa. These treaties made Tunisia a French protectorate, but much of the traditional system of government, including the position of the Bey, continued under French supervision.

Libya and the Senussiya

Early nineteenth century

The districts of Cyrenaica, Tripolitania and Fezzan, which today make up Libya, were in the eighteenth and early nineteenth centuries ruled by the Karamanli dynasty nominally as part of the Ottoman Empire. The largest port, Tripoli, was the northern terminus of important trans-Saharan trade routes from Hausaland and Borno. Attempts to suppress the trade in slaves led to considerable British interest in the area and during the reign of Yusuf Karamanli in the first decades of the nineteenth century, the British Consul at Tripoli, Warrington, exerted great influence. In the 1840s the British established consulates deep in the desert at Murzuk and Ghadames. During the 1830s the Ottoman sultans re-established their direct control over Tripoli and overthrew the Karamanlis. The Turkish governors had little power and their authority was not recognised in the interior districts such as Fezzan.

The Senussiya

These interior districts, and indeed most of the central Sahara, fell under the control of a Muslim brotherhood known as the Senussiya. Sayyid Mohammed al-Sanusi founded this brotherhood in 1837. Its headquarters were established in the desert of Cyrenaica, first at al-Baida, in 1843, then at Jughbub and finally from 1859 at the oasis of Kufra. From these centres al-Sanusi's followers spread out to found settlements known as 'zawiyas' throughout the Sahara. These developed into religious, educational, administrative and trading centres. In 1859 al-Sanusi was succeeded by his son, Mohammed al-Mahdi, and for the rest of the century the Senussiya were the dominant and stabilising influence over much of the desert. Under their protection the trade route from Wadai through Kufra to Benghazi became the most important of the trans-Saharan routes. The Turkish authorities on the coast recognised the power of the Senussiya and generally cooperated with them.

In 1911 the Italians conquered the coastal districts from the Turks, and from then on the Senussiya led a lengthy war of resistance against Italian rule.

5

The Western Sudan in the nineteenth century

The most important aspects of this topic are the jihads of Usman dan Fodio, Seku Ahmadu and al-Hajj Umar, the Mandinka Empire of Samori Toure, and the decline of Borno.

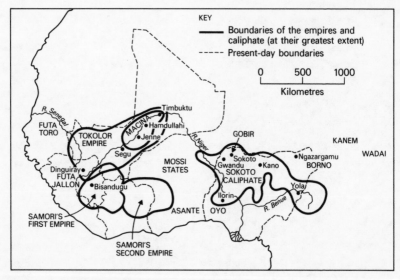

Map 6   The Western Sudan in the nineteenth century

The jihad of Usman dan Fodio

Main events

In 1800 throughout the Western Sudan Islam was a religion of a small minority and was often mixed with pre-Islamic ideas and customs. The Kanuri, Tuareg and Fulani were the most strongly Muslim and provided most of the scholars and teachers. It was these people, particularly the Fulani, who led the nineteenth-century jihads, the great reforming movements which revived and spread Islam. There were two main types of Fulani: the nomadic 'Bororoje' or Cattle Fulani and the settled 'Fulanin Gida' or Town Fulani. By 1800 both types lived through-out the Western Sudan with large concentrations in Hausaland, the Niger bend area and the Futa states.

The most important of the nineteenth-century jihads was that led by Usman dan Fodio in the first decades of the century. It transformed the divided, largely non-Muslim Hausa states into a large, united, Muslim, Fulani-ruled empire. Usman, a Fulani of the Toronkawa clan, lived in Gobir, the north-westernmost of the Hausa states. He advocated a return to pure Islam and condemned all non-Muslim practices. As his fame grew he attracted a large number of followers at his base at Degel. The Hausa rulers of Gobir were not devout Muslims and practised many of the abuses criticised by Usman, so it is not surprising that they regarded him as a threat to their power. In the last years of the eighteenth century the ruler of Gobir, Nafata, tried to reduce Usman's influence, and after 1802 his successor, Yunfa, continued the conflict. At the beginning of 1804 Yunfa threatened to attack Degel. On 21 February 1804 Usman and his followers fled from Degel to Gudu (thus making an 'hijira', just as the Prophet had done). Usman was proclaimed 'Amir-al-Muminin' (Commander of the Faithful) and a jihad was declared against the Hausa rulers.

In Gobir the jihad was a long, hard-fought war, the armies of Usman suffering several setbacks before the final victory was achieved with the fall of the Gobir capital, Alkalawa, in 1808. The jihad, however, was not confined to Gobir: Fulani in the other Hausa states rebelled against their rulers with the support of and acknowledging the authority of Usman.

By 1810 all the main Hausa states (e.g. Zaria, Katsina, Kano) had been conquered by the jihadists and new Fulani dynasties established. The western provinces of Borno (e.g. Gombe, Katagum) were also conquered, but two attempts to spread the jihad to the rest of Borno were defeated by the warrior-scholar al-Kanemi. Along the rivers Niger and Benue new Fulani emirates were founded in Nupe and Adamawa and further to the south the Fulani seized control of Ilorin and much of the Oyo Empire.

Causes of the jihad

The immediate cause of the jihad was the conflict in Gobir between Usman and Yunfa, but the long-term causes are more complex, involving religious, political and social factors.

a) Religious causes. Usman's main concern was the reform, purification and spread of Islam. Corruption, excessive taxation and non-Islamic practices existed throughout Hausaland and some areas such as Bauchi were still entirely non-Islamic. It was undoubtedly in many ways a religious revolt, a real jihad.

b) Political causes. The well-educated, strongly Muslim Fulanin Gida felt themselves largely excluded from political power and provided almost all the jihad leaders. The Cattle Fulani joined the jihad partly to escape the hated cattle tax ('jangali') and partly to assist their fellow Fulani. Therefore, although some Fulani supported the Hausa and many Hausa fought on the Fulani side, the jihad was partly a Fulani political revolt.

c) Social causes. Many of the Hausa peasantry (the 'talakawa') supported the jihad because of the injustice, oppressive rule and high taxation imposed on them by the Hausa rulers.

Why the jihad was successful

Several factors help to explain the rapid success of the jihadists.

a) The Hausa states lacked unity. For centuries there had been many wars between the Hausa states (e.g. during the late eighteenth century Gobir fought against Katsina, Kano and Zamfara). This weakened the Hausa states and prevented effective cooperation so that the jihadists could defeat them one by one.

b) The Hausa rulers could not rely on their subjects, many of whom supported the jihad hoping to see the end of high taxation and oppressive rule.

c) The jihad benefited greatly from the inspired leadership of Usman and his main supporters, especially his brother Abdullahi and his son and eventual successor Mohammed Bello.

d) The jihadists believed in what they were fighting for, and were convinced that they would go straight to paradise if killed while fighting the holy war.

e) The Fulani leaders cooperated with each other, all acknowledging the leadership of Usman as Commander of the Faithful.

Results of the jihad

a) Islam was purified, strengthened and spread throughout Hausaland. Without the jihad it is unlikely that Islam would have the dominant position it holds today in the area.

b) The old Hausa dynasties were overthrown and replaced by a single Fulani empire, ruled by Fulani emirs. On Usman's retirement in 1817, the empire was divided into two: his brother Abdullahi ruled the western half from Gwandu, while his son Mohammed Bello ruled the larger eastern half from Sokoto. Mohammed Bello succeeded to the title of Amir-al-Muminin and soon asserted his supremacy. He completed his father's work by preserving unity, suppressing rebellions and providing the empire with an efficient system of government which continued throughout the nineteenth century.

c) The creation of a strong, unified empire increased peace and stability which produced a great improvement in trade.

d) Education was increased and improved; Usman, Abdullahi and Mohammed Bello were all great scholars.

e) Usman's jihad influenced other jihads especially those of Seku Ahmadu about 1820 and al-Hajj Umar about 1850.

f) The attempts to spread the jihad to Borno led to the rise of al-Kanemi who reformed and strengthened Borno.

g) The spread of the jihad to Ilorin weakened the Oyo Empire and was a major cause of its collapse.

The jihad of Seku Ahmadu

The second of the nineteenth-century jihads was led by Seku Ahmadu, sometimes called Hamad Bari. The region affected was Macina, the inland delta area west of the Niger bend. The rulers of the area, the most important of whom was the

'Ardo' of Macina were Fulani of the Dyalo clan and they paid tribute to the non-Muslim Bambara king of Segu. Macina contained small Muslim minorities, but the rulers and most of the population were either not Muslim or Muslims who mixed Islam with traditional religion.

Seku Ahmadu was strongly influenced by the career of Usman dan Fodio and actually took part in the jihad in Gobir. When he returned to Macina he settled at Sebera, where he preached and gathered disciples. The Ardo grew so alarmed at Ahmadu's growing influence that he asked the king of Segu to help destroy him. Ahmadu made an hijira to Hamdullahi, proclaimed a jihad and was elected Amir al-Muminin.

After defeating the Segu army, Ahmadu was invited by the scholars of Jenne to rule their city and many Fulani chiefs joined the jihad, often for political reasons. After several years of fighting, Ahmadu ruled all of Macina and in 1819 he made Hamdullahi his capital. In 1826 Timbuktu was conquered but later rebelled against Fulani rule. Ahmadu made Macina a highly centralised, theocratic (the religious leaders holding political power) state. It was divided into five emirates and the central government was controlled by a Grand Council of forty and a Privy Council of three. Islam was firmly established and Islamic laws were strictly enforced (e.g. a censor of public morals was appointed).

The background and the causes of Ahmadu's jihad are very similar to those of Usman's jihad: a minority of devout Muslims wanted to overthrow a ruling class which ruled oppressively and contrary to the laws of Islam. In addition, in Macina, the jihad was partly a struggle between the Sangare clan of the Fulani and the ruling Fulani Dyalo, and partly a revolt of the masses against oppression and misrule. As in Hausaland the jihad was a civil war rather than an external invasion. The causes for success were also similar: on the one hand a weak, divided opposition and on the other strong, united support for the jihad. The later history of Macina was remarkably stable until Ahmadu III (Seku Ahmadu's grandson) was defeated and killed during the conquest of Macina by al-Hajj Umar in 1862.

The jihad of al-Hajj Umar

In the early nineteenth century the most important states between the bend of the Niger and the Atlantic were the non-Muslim Bambara states of Segu and Kaarta, the Muslim Futa states, small coastal kingdoms such as Cayor and many small non-Muslim Mandinka states. This area was transformed around the middle of the century by al-Hajj Umar, a Tokolor from Futa Toro.

As a young man, Umar spent many years on the pilgrimage to Mecca and on his return he visited Borno, Hausaland and Macina, learning from the Islamic reforms being carried out in those areas. At Mecca, Umar joined the Tijaniyya brotherhood and was appointed Caliph (leader) of the Tijaniyya in the Western Sudan. Umar's firm belief in the Tijaniyya brotherhood greatly influenced his career. Previously most Muslims in the Western Sudan had belonged to the ancient Qadiriyya brotherhood, which emphasised the importance of learning and favoured an elite of scholars. The more recently created Tijaniyya brotherhood stressed action rather than intellect, maintaining that Islam was a simple religion that all could easily understand and practice. This emphasis on equality made Tijaniyya ideas very attractive to ordinary people, and at several crucial points in Umar's career the conflict between the Qadiriyya and Tijaniyya proved to be important.

During the 1840s Umar preached widely in the Futa states and converted many from Qadiriyya to Tijaniyya Islam. The Qadiriyya 'Almamis', who had ruled the Futa states since eighteenth-century jihads, regarded Umar's Tijaniyya preaching as a threat to their own authority. In 1848 the Almami of Futa Jallon expelled Umar. He made an hijira to Dinguiray, large numbers of supporters joined him, and a jihad was proclaimed.

During the 1850s Umar created a large empire over which he imposed Tokolor rule and Tijaniyya Islam. From Dinguiray he attacked northwards and conquered the Bambara states of Bambuk and Kaarta. From the beginning Umar was in contact with the French on the Senegal coast, and from them he acquired guns. Both the French and the rulers of the Futa states were alarmed by the creation and rapid growth of the Tokolor Empire. In 1854 Faidherbe became Governor of the French coastal settlements and expanded French power in the lower Senegal valley. In 1855 there was conflict between Umar and the French over Fort Medina: Umar was prevented from expanding down the Senegal valley and so turned eastwards. In 1861 Umar conquered the powerful Bambara state of Segu and then moved against Macina, the creation of Seku Ahmadu's earlier jihad. His arguments for attacking Muslim Macina were similar to those used by Usman dan Fodio to justify his attack on Borno. Ahmadu III of Macina had allied with the non-Muslim king of Segu and therefore deserved to be treated as a non-Muslim. Moreover the Tijaniyya Muslims had little sympathy for Qadiriyya Macina. Umar conquered Macina in 1862, but was killed during a rebellion there two years later.

Umar was succeeded as ruler of the Tokolor Empire by his son, Ahmadu, who faced many problems (e.g. rebellions). As soon as Ahmadu had solved these internal problems, he was faced with an external threat, from the French. During the late 1870s the French began to expand further up the Senegal valley and during the 1880s conquered the whole of the Tokolor Empire. Although Umar's empire was short-lived, his religious achievements were lasting: Tijaniyya Islam still remains the dominant religion of the area.

The Mandinka Empire of Samori Toure

Around the middle of the nineteenth century, the area south and east of the headwaters of the Niger inhabited by the Mandinka people was divided into many small states, the most important of which were Kankan, Odienne, and Sikasso. Most of the Mandinka still practised their traditional religion, although there were some Muslims, especially among the Diula long-distance traders. Samori Toure, who began as a trader, soon became a military leader and during the 1850s and 1860s he created a large empire centred on his capital, Bisandugu. In 1873 he conquered Kankan and assumed the title of Almami, for throughout his career Samori did everything possible to spread Tijaniyya Islam.

He provided his empire with a unique and highly effective political and military organisation. The villages were grouped into cantons which in turn were grouped into ten provinces. At each level, authority was shared by the traditional rulers, the military and the religious leaders; e.g. each canton was ruled by a chief, a military administrator and a 'qadi' (Muslim judge). The central government was controlled by the Almami assisted by a state council. A standing army of between two and three thousand soldiers (known as the 'sofa') was established. This well-trained and well-equipped army was paid for largely by a tax on gold and by the sale of slaves. From the early 1880s Samori used this army to fight a long guerrilla war against the French.

Nineteenth-century Borno

Effects of the jihad of Usman dan Fodio

At the beginning of the nineteenth century, the Borno Empire was still the strongest power in the Central Sudan. The ruler, known as the 'Mai', belonged to the Sefawa dynasty and lived in seclusion as a semi-divine king. A state council of twelve and administrators known as 'Kokenawa' provided stable, efficient, Islamic government.

When the jihad of Usman dan Fodio began in the Hausa states, Borno sent assistance to some of the Hausa states. This encouraged Fulani leaders (e.g. Gwani Muktar and Ibrahim Zaki) in Borno's western provinces to fight jihads and establish Fulani emirates (e.g. Hadejia, Gombe). In 1808 the Fulani jihadists captured the Borno capital, Ngazargamu, and at the same time Borno's eastern neighbour, Wadai, conquered Bagirmi and threatened Kanem. In this crisis the Mai turned for help to a Shuwa Arab scholar, al-Kanemi. Al-Kanemi drove the Fulani jihadists out of central Borno in 1808 and again when they invaded a second time in 1811, and in the process became the real power in Borno.

From then until his death in 1837 al-Kanemi with the title of Shehu increased his authority and seriously threatened the power of the Mai. From the new capital at Kuka, he reformed the system of government and re-established Borno's control over Zinder, Kanem and Bagirmi. In 1837 he was succeeded by his son, Shehu Umar, and by the 1840s there was great rivalry between the Shehu and the Mai. This led to civil war in 1846, in which Mai Ibrahim was killed marking the end of the Sefawa dynasty. Shehu Umar became full ruler of Borno.

The decline of Borno

Several factors help to explain Borno's rapid decline after 1840.
a) Rivalry between the largely Shuwa Arab supporters of the Shehus and the largely Kanuri supporters of the Mais culminating in the civil war of the 1840s greatly weakened Borno.
b) Borno's western provinces were lost to the Sokoto Caliphate, and the growth of this Caliphate made the trans-Saharan trade routes from Kano and Katsina more important than those starting in Borno.
c) Even more important was the growth of Wadai which conquered Kanem and Bagirmi from Borno in the 1840s. Wadai cooperated closely with the Senussiya brotherhood and by the last decades of the century the Wadai-

Benghazi route was the most important trans-Saharan trade route.

By the 1880s Borno was a weak state struggling to survive between two more powerful neighbours. Borno's weakness was shown by the ease with which it was conquered in the 1890s by Rabeh, an adventurer from the Eastern Sudan.

6

West African coastal states in the nineteenth century

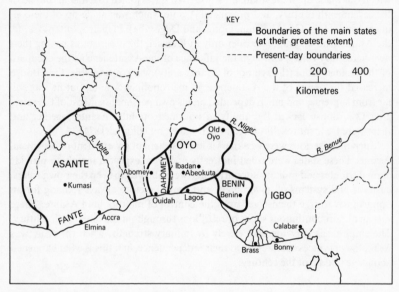

Map 7   West African coastal states

Asante

The reign of Osei Bonsu

The Asante Empire reached the peak of its power during the reign of Asantehene Osei Bonsu in the first decades of the nineteenth century (1801–24). He continued the constitutional reforms of his predecessor, Osei Kwadwo, suppressed all rebellions and enlarged the empire. In a series of wars between 1806 and 1824 he conquered the coastal Fante states. Many factors had for long made relations between the Fante and Asante hostile.

a) The Fante would not allow the Asante to trade directly with the Europeans at the coast.

b) The Asante needed regular supplies of guns from the European traders and could not allow their supply routes to be at the mercy of the Fante.

c) The Fante helped Asante's southern provinces (e.g. Akyem, Denkyira) whenever they rebelled against Asante control.

Shortly after his final defeat of Fante in 1824 Osei Bonsu died. His successors proved unable to maintain the empire intact; during the next fifty years the Asante Empire collapsed almost completely.

Causes for the decline of the Asante Empire: the system of government

One main cause for the decline of Asante was weakness in the empire's system of government. The empire comprised two distinct parts: metropolitan Asante which was made up of the small, mostly Oyoko states joined together at the end of the seventeenth century, and provincial Asante which was made up of the con-quered states (e.g. Ga, Akwamu, Gonja and Dagomba). In metropolitan Asante, the Asantehene was supreme ruler only in Kumasi, the other states having their own hereditary rulers, although the influence of the Asantehene as the occupant of the Golden Stool (the symbol of Asante unity) was considerable. Osei Bonsu increased the power of the Asantehene in metropolitan Asante, but he was still far from supreme, and much depended on his own personality. Most of the rulers after Osei Bonsu lacked the ability to hold metropolitan Asante together and there were frequent rebellions (e.g. the Dwaben rebellion of 1874).

Much more serious were weaknesses in the system of government of provincial Asante. These states were ruled indirectly and were expected merely to provide annual tributes and military support. They were allowed to keep their own rulers, customs and systems of government and were therefore always looking for an opportunity to free themselves from the control of metropolitan Asante. There was an almost continuous series of rebellions throughout the nineteenth century. The empire was kept together purely by military strength; when the army was weak, the provinces soon regained their independence, and this is what happened about the middle of the century.

Causes for the decline of the Asante Empire: conflict with the British

On several occasions during the nineteenth century, the Asante fought the British on the coast. It was these wars which eventually destroyed the military power of Asante and led to the break-up of the empire. These wars had several causes.

a) The Asante were mainly concerned with suppressing rebellions among their southern tributaries (e.g. Akyem, Denkyira).

b) The Asante were determined to keep the coastal trading fort of Elmina, their main source for the supply of guns. Their invasions of the coast around 1870 were largely an attempt to prevent Elmina falling into the hands of the British after the departure of the Dutch.

c) The British always supported the coastal states, especially the Fante, against the Asante because they feared the effects on trade of a powerful Asante reaching the coast.

d) British traders encouraged the destruction of Asante in order to open up trade with the interior.

e) The missionaries also wanted the Asante driven from the coast.

Decisive defeats of Asante by the British (e.g. in 1826 and 1874) led to the break-up of the empire and the Asante were forced to recognise the independence of their southern states by the Fomena treaty of 1874. The wars encouraged the Fante to unite, culminating in the short-lived Fante Confederation created in 1868. This was rapidly weakened by the British who established the Crown Colony of the Gold Coast in 1874. With the accession of Prempe as Asantehene in 1888, the power of Asante began to revive, but in 1896 the British conquered Asante, exiled Prempe and declared a protectorate over the whole area.

Dahomey

In 1821 Gezo, King of Dahomey, was able to take advantage of the weakness of Oyo to break free of Oyo completely. Gezo in the first half of the nineteenth century, and his successors, Glele and Behanzin, in the second half, ruled a strong, unified kingdom which kept its strength long after Oyo and Asante had collapsed. Several wars were fought against the western Yoruba provinces of Ketu and Abeokuta to gain control of more of the palm belt. Several factors help to explain the survival of Dahomey as a strong kingdom until the last decade of the century.

a) Dahomey was small in size and therefore it was reasonably easy to preserve its unity, in comparison to the larger Oyo and Asante Empires.

b) The kingdom was highly centralised with all conquered peoples fully integrated. Unlike most West African states Dahomey did not have the problem of being surrounded by discontented vassal states always rebelling and struggling for independence.

c) The King was a semi-divine, absolute monarch controlling every aspect of the life of the kingdom and commanding absolute respect.

d) Dahomey possessed an effective system of succession to the throne and thus avoided numerous succession disputes.

e) Assisting the king were several officials (e.g. the Migan, Meu and Yevogan) with clearly-defined areas of responsibility and a highly efficient bureaucracy.

f) Dahomey possessed a large, well-organised standing army.

g) The kingdom possessed sufficient revenue from customs duties and from taxes on income and agriculture. The final abolition of the slave trade around the middle of the nineteenth century seriously affected the economy, but a largely successful effort was made to replace trade in slaves with trade in palm-oil.

h) Unlike Oyo and Asante, Dahomey did not suffer any serious external threats until the 1890s.

During the 1880s the French established themselves in Cotonou and Porto Novo, and in 1894 a powerful French army conquered Dahomey and exiled Behanzin, the last king of independent Dahomey.

Oyo

The fall of Oyo

The large Oyo Empire, which was at the height of its power in the eighteenth century, had completely collapsed by the middle of the nineteenth century. The city of Old Oyo had been burnt and abandoned, Dahomey and many of the Yoruba states were independent, and much of central Oyo had become part of the Sokoto Caliphate as the Fulani emirate of Ilorin. The following are the main causes for the fall of Oyo.

a) The military strength of Oyo declined towards the end of the eighteenth century (e.g. Oyo was defeated by the Nupe).

b) There was economic decline caused by the interruption of the northern trade routes by the rise of Nupe and the wars connected with the jihad in Hausaland and a decline in the slave trade on the coast.

c) Largely as a result of European contact on the coast, the southern part of the empire was overtaking the north as the economic and cultural centre of influence, thus making it unlikely that the north would be able to continue its political supremacy for long.

d) At the beginning of the nineteenth century Oyo was challenged by the rise of powerful neighbours (e.g. Dahomey and Nupe).

e) Oyo's complex system of government began to break down. At the head of the government was the Alafin whose powers were checked by a council known as the 'Oyo Mesi' (headed by the chief minister, the 'Bashorun') and the Ogboni society. There were no strong Alafins after the death of Abiodun in 1789 and the activities of Bashorun Gaha in the 1760s upset the constitutional balance.

f) The immediate, and perhaps most important, cause for the fall of Oyo was a complete breakdown in the central government after the death of Abiodun. When Alafin Awole tried to attack an Ife town, the army and most of the great officials refused to obey him and forced him to commit suicide. After him there were two short-lived Alafins and then for a long period the Oni of Ife (ruler of the Yoruba mother-state of Ife) refused to install any Alafin. Many chiefs used this opportunity to increase their own power and when a new Alafin was finally appointed many refused to recognise his authority.

g) Recovery from this internal collapse might have been possible had it not been for an external threat, the spread of the Fulani jihad to Ilorin. In 1817 the Kakanfo (army commander) Afonja, in an attempt to create a kingdom for himself, asked the Fulani under Alimi for help. Alimi soon took over control and Ilorin became part of the Sokoto Caliphate. The Fulani tried to push the jihad further south and in 1837 attacked and destroyed the city of Old Oyo.

h) In the confusion of the first decades of the nineteenth century many parts of the empire (e.g. Dahomey) broke free. The Owu war which started in about 1813 was the first of a long series of civil wars in which the successor states of Oyo struggled to establish their position in the new system.

Yoruba wars

Yorubaland experienced a series of civil wars throughout most of the nineteenth

36

century and also invasions from the Fulani from the north and by Dahomey from the west. The collapse of Oyo created a power vacuum which many states fought to fill; by the middle of the century Ibadan was the most powerful state, but the wars continued as the other states tried to limit Ibadan's imperial ambitions. Economic competition as well as political rivalries helped to cause the wars; the southern states fought to control the trade routes to the coast, as the supply of firearms was becoming increasingly important. These wars can be divided into three main periods.

a) 1813–37. The main events were:
- the collapse of Oyo.
- Afonja's revolt in Ilorin and Fulani involvement.
- the Owu war in the south.
- large-scale migrations southwards and the founding of new cities (e.g. Ibadan, Abeokuta and new Oyo).

b) 1837–78. The main events were:
- the struggle between Oyo's successor states, especially Ibadan and Abeokuta, which reached its height during the Ijaye war (1860–65).
- the defeat of the Fulani by Ibadan at Oshogbo in 1840 and the weakening of the Fulani threat.
- the beginning of invasions by Dahomey (e.g. their attacks on Abeokuta in 1851 and 1864).
- the beginning of British intervention when troops from the newly-created colony of Lagos were sent against the Egba in 1865.

c) 1878–93. The main events were:
- most of the Yoruba states allied together to check the growth of Ibadan (the Ekiti wars).
- in 1892 the British decisively defeated Ijebu.
- in 1893 the British Governor of Lagos, Carter, persuaded the Yoruba states to stop fighting and arranged treaties of protection.

The Igbo and the Delta states

The Igbo

The Igbo provide a good example of a segmentary society (one with no large-scale, centralised political institutions). The Igbo were divided into patrilinear clans each tracing themselves back to a common ancestor. Igboland was densely populated with thousands of village groups, each ruling itself. The fact that each unit was reasonably small made a very democratic form of government possible.

There were two main institutions of government in each village: the 'Ama-ala' or Council of Elders and the village assembly. The Ama-ala was usually composed of the heads of each extended family, but in the village assembly all had the right to speak and decisions had to be unanimous. The system of justice was equally democratic and age-set organisations were used to undertake public works. Among the Ibibio and Cross River Igbo secret societies were common, the most powerful of which was the Ekpe society.

Some links did exist between the different village groups. Most of the Igbo recognised the same gods and there were some oracles, especially that at Aro-

37

chukwu, which commanded respect throughout Igboland. The Aro, largely as a result of their role as guardians of the oracle, dominated the long-distance trade routes, supplying first slaves and later palm-oil to the coastal towns (e.g. Bonny, Calabar).

The Delta city-states

The Niger Delta city-states (e.g. Bonny, Brass) were major participants first in the slave trade and later in the palm-oil trade. The change-over from slaves to palm-oil around the middle of the nineteenth century was, in most cases, successfully accomplished, but was accompanied by great political changes and increasing European involvement. Each state possessed a royal family (e.g. the Pepples of Bonny) and a number of 'Houses', which were a kind of trading corporation which had developed out of lineage groups. A new class of men, including many ex-slaves, changed over to the palm-oil trade earlier than the traditional house leaders and soon gained control of the Houses.

From the 1860s onwards there was fierce competition for control of the palm-oil trade. Both the number of European companies and the number of states wanting a share in the trade increased (e.g. Jaja and his followers left Bonny in the 1860s and founded the new state of Opobo). As competition in trade increased so did European, especially British, involvement in the internal affairs of the Delta states. The amalgamation of all the British trading companies in the area into the Royal Niger Company in the early 1880s led to a great increase in British activity in the Niger area and the British Government showed itself more and more willing to support the interests of its traders.

7

Central Africa in the nineteenth century

The Congo forests and further north

At the beginning of the nineteenth century this was the part of Africa least affected by external influences. Much of the area was covered by dense rain forest, population was thinly distributed, long-distance trade was little developed and few political organisations existed larger than villages. This relative isolation and lack of state-formation help to explain the absence of detailed historical information until the last decades of the century. The dominant theme in the nineteenth-century history of most peoples in this area was increasing pressure from outsiders linked with the growth of trade in slaves and ivory.

The peoples north of the Congo forests (present-day northern Cameroon, the Central African Republic and Chad) were greatly influenced by pressures from the north, east and west. To the east of Lake Chad, the state of Wadai grew in strength and became increasingly involved in the Arab-Muslim trade of northern Africa. Wadai prospered from the export of large numbers of slaves to North Africa until the whole area was thrown into confusion by Rabeh in the 1890s. In the north-east the peoples of the Nile-Congo watershed (e.g. the Azande) were from about the middle of the century coming into conflict with Arab slave-traders from Turco-Egyptian Sudan. In the west the many small chiefdoms of central and northern Cameroon (e.g. Tikar, Mbum and Bamum) were disrupted by Fulani jihadists trying to extend Adamawa, the easternmost emirate of the Sokoto Caliphate.

The largest group of people in the coastal area between the Cameroon Mountains and the mouth of the Congo were the Fang or Pahouin. During the early nineteenth century they were still expanding southwards to occupy much of the coastal forests. They lived in a segmentary society and were the most important suppliers of ivory to the European traders on the coast. Europeans of many nations had for long traded at Duala, Loango and Cabinda, and new trading stations were established during the second half of the century (e.g. by the French on the Gabon coast). As the slave trade declined, ivory became the most important article of trade. In the area to the north of the lower Congo, trade was dominated by the Vili people around Loango and by the Teke.

Most of the peoples living in the dense forests of the northern Congo basin (e.g. the Mongo) lived in small, independent village communities. Some ivory and other forest products filtered down the Congo and its tributaries towards the coast, but the rapids and hilly country along the last three hundred kilometres of the Congo (from present-day Kinshasa to the coast) limited the development of trade. It was not until Stanley's journey of 1877 that Europeans became aware

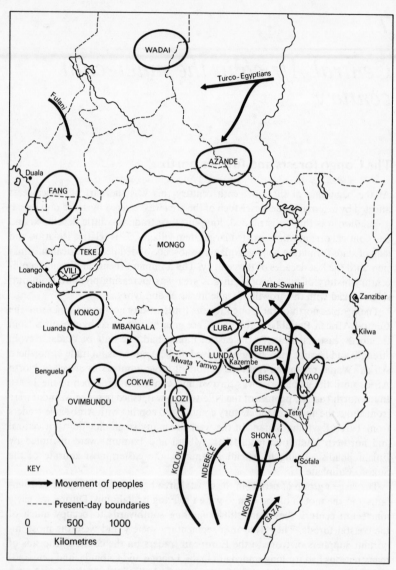

Map 8   Nineteenth century central Africa

of the navigational potential of the Congo and its tributaries and the lower Congo
became one of the main areas of European interest and rivalry in Africa.

The coastal areas south of the Congo

The many different peoples of this area (present-day Angola, south-western

Zaïre and western Zambia) were greatly affected during the nineteenth century by the growth of trade between the interior and the Portuguese settlements on the coast. The Portuguese used African trading agents, the 'pombeiros', to trade with the peoples of the interior, especially the Imbangala of Kasanje and further south the Ovimbundu. These two peoples controlled the trade routes to the many Luba-Lunda states in the centre of the continent. At the beginning of the century, trade in slaves was most important, but the Portuguese loss of Brazil and their official prohibition of the slave trade in 1836 caused ivory to replace slaves as the major article of trade by mid-century. Other tropical products, especially rubber, became important from the 1870s onwards.

In the early years of the century the most important trade route was controlled by the Imbangala and ran from Luanda on the coast eastwards through Kasanje to the great Lunda kingdom of the Mwata Yamvo in what is now south-western Zaïre. The Mwata Yamvo also traded eastwards with the Kazembe kingdom which was linked by Bisa and Yao traders with the Portuguese on the lower Zambezi. The decline of the slave trade weakened the Imbangala and by the middle of the century their southern neighbours, the Ovimbundu, were the most important traders in the area.

Under Ovimbundu control, most of the trade from the interior followed more southerly routes to the coast at Benguela rather than to Luanda. The Ovimbundu were well-placed to control the ivory trade because their eastern neighbours were the Cokwe, the greatest ivory hunters of the area. With a plentiful supply of guns, the Cokwe brought larger and larger areas under their control in their search for ivory. In 1885 the kingdom of the Mwata Yamvo was destroyed by the Cokwe and by the 1890s they controlled most of what is now eastern Angola and south-western Zaïre. The rise of the Ovimbundu and Cokwe and the collapse of the Mwata Yamvo kingdom illustrate the contrasting effects of the growth of trade on different peoples. Trade brought some benefits like the spread of new food crops (e.g. cassava), but also spread guns, warfare and slave-raiding. Those controlling the trade routes (e.g. the Cokwe) gained the most guns and became more powerful, while once-great kingdoms further from the coast (e.g. the Lunda states) declined. Despite several attempts, the Portuguese failed to extend their authority far inland until the last decade of the century.

Central African states

In the centre of the southern half of Africa (the present-day countries of southern Zaïre, Zambia, Malawi and Zimbabwe) several large, well-organised states existed long before the nineteenth century. Many of these states used Luba and Lunda political ideas (such as semi-divine, hereditary kingship) and their royal families were often of Luba or Lunda origin. These states had trading links with both the west and east coasts. In the early years of the nineteenth century, the Zambezi valley was the most important trade route between the interior and the east coast. The Portuguese had been established on the Mozambique coast since the sixteenth century and their trading settlements (e.g. Sena, Tete and Zumbo) along the Zambezi traded with the peoples north and south of the middle Zambezi. By the middle of the century, however, more northerly trade routes to the

Swahili cities of the east coast (e.g. Kilwa) were more important than the old Zambezi routes. Slaves and ivory were the most important articles of trade and some peoples (e.g. the Bisa and the Yao) became specialists in long-distance trade and controlled most of the trade routes. The following were among the most important states and peoples in the area during the nineteenth century.

a) Mwata Yamvo. This Lunda state (Mwata Yamvo was the name of the capital and the title of the ruler) was probably the strongest and largest state in central Africa at the beginning of the century, controlling large areas along the upper Kasai and Lulua Rivers from the edge of the Congo forests southwards to the headwaters of the Zambezi. By mid-century the kingdom had been weakened by frequent succession disputes and was unable to survive the attacks of the better-armed Cokwe in the 1880s.

b) Kazembe. This eastern Lunda kingdom was in origin an offshoot of Mwata Yamvo, but by the nineteenth century was independent of and as strong as its parent-state. It covered a large area on both sides of the River Luapula (parts of present-day Shaba region of Zaïre and north-east Zambia) including rich deposits of copper. It survived as a powerful state trading in slaves and ivory until greatly weakened by Msiri and his Nyamwezi followers in the 1860s.

c) Bemba. The Bemba people lived in the area between Kazembe and Lake Malawi (north-eastern Zambia). During the nineteenth century the Bemba gained increasing control of the Bisa trade routes, acquired guns and grew stronger, especially during the reign of Chitimukulu Citapankwa (1866–87).

d) Lozi. In the flood-plains of the upper Zambezi (western Zambia) the Lozi had established a large, well-organised kingdom. Most of the Lozi state was conquered in the late 1830s by the Kololo led by Sebitwane. (See Chapter 9.) Under Sebitwane the Lozi and Kololo lived in harmony and prospered, but his successor Sekeletu (1851–65) was unpopular and unable to maintain unity. In 1865 the Lozi led by Sepopa rebelled against the Kololo and restored Lozi rule.

e) Shona and Ndebele. In 1800 the area south of the middle Zambezi (present-day Zimbabwe) was still controlled by the Shona states of Mwene Mutapa (smaller and weaker than in earlier centuries) and the Rozwi confederacy ruled by the Changamire dynasty. Both states were destroyed in the 1830s by Ngoni invasions from the south, leaving the area defenceless against another influx of people from the south displaced by the Mfecane, the Ndebele. Led by Mzilikazi, the Ndebele conquered much of present-day Zimbabwe in the 1840s and established a strong Zulu-type state. (See Chapter 9.)

f) Malawi area. The many different peoples living in the Lake Malawi area (e.g. the Yao and Cewa) were thrown into confusion by the invasions of different groups of Ngoni in the 1840s and 1850s. This area was particularly badly affected by slave raiders from the east coast throughout the century.

The impact of traders from East Africa

Much of Central Africa from Lake Malawi northwards into the Congo forests was greatly affected in the second half of the nineteenth century by traders from East Africa. These traders were Swahili from the trading cities of the east coast (controlled by the Omani Sultan of Zanzibar) and Nyamwezi from around Tabora (present-day central Tanzania). The increasing demand for ivory and slaves in the 1830s and 1840s encouraged these traders to go further and further into the interior. Their use of guns and groups of mercenaries (known as 'rugaruga') enabled them to cause great devastation and to conquer large areas. The methods and effects of these traders are best illustrated by the careers of two of the most successful of them, Msiri and Tippu Tip.

Msiri

From the 1840s Swahili and Nyamwezi traders were increasingly interested in the copper and ivory of the Kazembe kingdom. In 1856 a Nyamwezi trader called Msiri and his followers settled at Bunkeya in the centre of what is now the Shaba region of Zaïre. With the help of his Nyamwezi followers, known as the Bayeke, Msiri soon controlled most of the trade west to Mwata Yamvo and Angola and east to Zanzibar. By the 1870s the Lunda state of Kazembe and the Luba state further north had virtually collapsed and most of their territory was ruled by Msiri. His power lasted until the area was invaded by the Belgians and Msiri was killed in 1891.

Tippu Tip

Swahili traders first crossed Lake Tanganyika into the southern fringes of the Zaïre forests in about 1840. Using methods similar to those of Msiri, these traders soon had great influence over a wide area. Hamed bin Mohammed, better known as Tippu Tip, was part Swahili and part Nyamwezi. During his early career he traded in the Nyamwezi and Kazembe areas, but in the late 1860s he moved further north establishing his main centre at Kasongo on the Lualaba River. He soon united the Swahili traders in the area under his control, conquered most of the peoples in the Lomami and Lualaba valleys and for over twenty years was the most powerful ruler in the eastern Congo. The search for ivory and slaves caused great destruction throughout the area. Tippu Tip regarded himself as a subject of the Sultan of Zanzibar, but in the late 1880s he was forced to accept Belgian control, and he spent his last years in the Congo as an agent of the Belgians.

8

East Africa in the nineteenth century

The most important aspects of this topic are the Omani Empire (especially the achievements of Sayyid Said), the growth of trade with the interior (especially Mirambo and the Nyamwezi), the Ngoni invasions and developments in the interlacustrine kingdoms (especially Buganda).

The Omani Empire

The reign of Sultan Sayyid Said

In 1800 most of the trading cities of the east coast were ruled by Swahili families, the most powerful of which were the Mazrui of Mombasa. These cities had for long had close connections with Oman (in south-eastern Arabia), but it was not until the reign of Sayyid Said (1806–56) that Omani rule was firmly established along the coast. After unsuccessful attempts to expand his power in Arabia in the early years of his reign, Sayyid Said increasingly concentrated on the coast of East Africa. He was a trader and diplomat of genius and, by the time of his death in 1856, his capital, Zanzibar, was the centre of a huge commercial empire.

The following were the main achievements of Sayyid Said.

a) Control of the coast. By skilful diplomacy and the use of military and naval strength Sayyid Said gradually asserted Omani control over the trading cities of the east coast. During the 1820s the Mazrui rulers of Mombasa gained temporary British support against Sayyid Said and were not finally conquered until 1837. By 1840 Sayyid Said loosely controlled all the main coastal cities from Mogadishu in the north to Kilwa in the south.

b) Development of Zanzibar. In 1840 Sayyid Said made Zanzibar his capital. During his reign Zanzibar grew rapidly and became the most important commercial centre in East Africa. It has been estimated that about 40,000 slaves a year were being sold in Zanzibar in the 1840s. Plantation agriculture was encouraged and Zanzibar and the neighbouring island of Pemba were soon the world's largest producers of cloves (a valuable spice).

c) Economic policies. The growth of trade was Sayyid Said's main concern. Customs duties were simplified and made more efficient and a new currency was introduced. Indian businessmen and bankers were encouraged to settle in Zanzibar and provided most of the capital to finance large-scale trade.

d) Diplomacy. One of Sayyid Said's greatest qualities was the ability to encourage many different groups (Arab, African, Indian and European) to work together to promote trade.

e) Trade with the interior. It was during his reign that Arab trading caravans

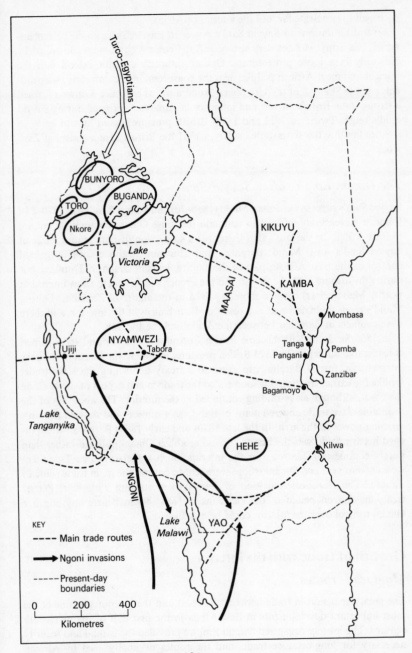

Map 9   Nineteenth century East Africa

began to penetrate far into the interior of Africa.

Several limitations to Sayyid Said's power in East Africa should be remembered. His army was not very strong and the coastal cities were controlled by him only in a loose protectorate. Omani authority did not extend into the interior and most African peoples near the coast remained completely independent, e.g. the Shamba of the Usambara Mountains, whose ruler Kimweri formed a strong state. British interest and influence in Zanzibar increased during Sayyid Said's reign. Twice (in 1822 and 1845) British pressure forced him to agree to treaties limiting the slave trade and from 1841 the British kept a consul at Zanzibar.

The Omani Empire after Sayyid Said

Sayyid Said's successors, Sultan Majid (1856–70) and Sultan Barghash (1870–88), found it increasingly difficult to maintain the loose Omani commercial empire in East Africa. In the late 1850s there was a succession dispute among three of Sayyid Said's sons, Majid, Barghash and Thuwain. Majid eventually gained control of the East African part of the empire, leaving Oman to Thuwain, but during the dispute both the British and the French (beginning to show interest in nearby Madagascar) became more involved in the affairs of Zanzibar. During Majid's reign trade declined as a result of disturbances in the interior, and there were conflicts in Zanzibar between the Arabs and the Indians.

In 1866 Sir John Kirk became British Consul at Zanzibar and soon gained considerable influence. In 1873 British pressure, including the threat of military intervention, forced Barghash to agree to a treaty abolishing the slave trade. Unlike the earlier treaties, this soon ended the trade in and export of slaves along the coast, although slave-raiding continued in the interior. The abolition of the profitable slave trade angered many of Barghash's subjects and showed Britain's growing power in the area. In the late 1870s and early 1880s Barghash strengthened his army and was the first to try and establish Omani political rather than purely commercial control over the interior. Such trader-rulers as Tippu Tip were encouraged, and Omani troops were sent to control the main trade route to Tabora. The European partition of East Africa, starting with Karl Peters' treaty-making on behalf of the Germans in 1884, began before any effective Omani control over the interior could be established.

Growth of trade with the interior

Main trade routes

The great expansion in trade between the coast and the interior was one of the most important developments in East Africa in the first half of the nineteenth century. The loosely-organised Omani Empire provided the capital and security necessary for long-distance trade, and the routes originally used by African traders were increasingly taken over and expanded by large Arab-led caravans. This expansion was the result of a great increase in demand for both slaves and ivory. There had for long been a small trade in slaves from the east coast to Arabia and the Persian Gulf, but in the first half of the nineteenth century three new markets for slaves developed. The French needed slaves to work on the plantations in their Indian Ocean islands (especially Réunion). The Portuguese started exporting more slaves to America from East Africa when the British made the slave trade from West Africa more difficult. Large numbers of slaves were needed to work the clove plantations of Zanzibar and Pemba. Even greater was the increase in European and American demand for ivory, which by 1850 was a more important item of trade than slaves.

By 1850 three main trade routes can be distinguished.

a) The southern route ran from ports such as Kilwa and Lindi to the area around Lake Malawi. The Yao were the African people most involved in trade on this route. This was the only route almost entirely concerned with trade in slaves and throughout the century Arab and Yao slave-raiders caused great devastation among the weak, segmentary societies between Lake Malawi and the coast (present-day southern Tanzania).

b) The central route, probably the most important, ran from such ports as Bagamoyo, Pangani and Tanga on the coast opposite Zanzibar (known as the 'Mrima' coast) to Tabora from where routes ran south-westwards to Kazembe and Msiri's area of influence, westwards to Lake Tanganyika and the Congo forests, and northwards to Lake Victoria and the interlacustrine kingdoms. Several large Arab trading settlements developed along these routes (e.g. Tabora and Ujiji). Ivory was more important than slaves and the Nyamwezi played a major part in the trade.

c) Less important were the northern routes from such ports as Tanga and Mombasa into the interior of what is now Kenya. Trade, mostly in ivory, was almost completely controlled by the Kamba people and the hostility of powerful groups such as the Maasai and Kikuyu prevented any Arab penetration until the 1860s.

Only in a few areas did Arab traders succeed in exerting any political control, but the effects of the development of long-distance trade were widespread. Islam and the Swahili language were introduced to many peoples and large quantities of guns were imported.

Mirambo and the Nyamwezi

The Nyamwezi people living in the area which is now north-western Tanzania were greatly affected by the growth of trade. At the beginning of the nineteenth century the Nyamwezi were divided into many small groups and were starting to trade with the coast. In the 1820s Arab traders established a commercial settlement at Tabora in the Nyamwezi chiefdom of Unyanyembe and by the 1850s largely controlled the area and its trade routes. During the 1860s Mirambo, chief of a small Nyamwezi group, began to build up his military strength and united the Nyamwezi under his rule. By 1870 his capital at Urambo was as important a trading centre as Tabora. The Arabs fought hard to retain control of the trade routes, but in 1876 were forced to recognise Mirambo's strength and trade on his terms. Using groups of well-armed mercenaries Mirambo established a strong Nyamwezi state (known as Urambo) which controlled most of the trade from the interior to the coast. Mirambo died in 1884 and the state he had created soon collapsed.

The Ngoni invasions

Much of the southern half of East Africa was greatly disturbed around the middle of the nineteenth century by Ngoni invasions. The Ngoni were originally warriors from southern Africa whose migrations were part of the general upheaval known as the Mfecane. The largest Ngoni group, led by Zwangendaba, crossed the Zambezi in 1835 and settled in the Fipa district (between Lake Malawi and Lake Tanganyika) in about 1840. During their long march north the Ngoni had absorbed into their group the remnants of many peoples that had been conquered. Their use of Zulu-type military tactics introduced new methods of warfare into East Africa.

After Zwangendaba's death in 1848, the Ngoni split into several groups and moved out of the Fipa area. Some groups (e.g. the Ngoni led by Mpezeni) moved south-westwards into what is now Malawi and eastern Zambia. The Tuta Ngoni moved north along the eastern shores of Lake Tanganyika disturbing the trade routes and weakening the Nyamwezi during the 1850s. The rise of Mirambo was assisted by both the weakening of many Nyamwezi chiefs and the introduction of new tactics. Another Ngoni group, known as the Gwangara, moved south-east to the Songea district just north of the Rovuma river). There they met the Maseko Ngoni, who had been moving north during the 1830s through what is now Mozambique. They drove out the Maseko and established a Ngoni state in Songea, from which they raided the whole area from Lake Malawi to the coast for the rest of the century.

The wanderings and wars of these different groups of Ngoni spread conflict and destruction over wide areas. Some who had been defeated by the Ngoni and had lost their lands and homes formed themselves into groups of plundering warriors (known as 'ruga-ruga' or 'maviti') who spread war and destruction over an even wider area. To preserve themselves from Ngoni attacks, some peoples adopted Ngoni tactics and united into strong centralised states. Mirambo and the Nyamwezi provide one example of this process. An even better example is the creation of the Hehe state: from the 1860s onwards two great leaders, Muyugumba and Mkwawa, succeeded in uniting the previously much-divided Hehe people into a strong state.

The interlacustrine kingdoms

The interlacustrine region (meaning the area between the lakes) is today occupied by the southern half of Uganda and the north-western corner of Tanzania, the area north and west of Lake Victoria. This was the only part of East Africa where strong, centralised states existed from a very early period, for example the small kingdoms of the Zinza and Haya people and the larger states of Bunyoro, Buganda, Toro, Nkore and Rwanda. The most powerful of these interlacustrine kingdoms in the nineteenth century were Buganda and Bunyoro.

Buganda

The fertile, densely populated kingdom of Buganda along the north-west shores of Lake Victoria had by 1800 emerged as the strongest of the interlacustrine kingdoms. It was a highly centralised state with very great powers in the hands of its ruler, known as the 'kabaka'. During the middle decades of the nineteenth century Buganda reached the height of its power under two very able kabakas, Suna II and Mutesa I. These rulers strengthened Buganda and the powers of the kabaka by reorganising the army, introducing the use of guns, raiding for slaves, ivory and cattle, expanding trade, and weakening the authority of all who might limit the absolute powers of the kabaka. Arabs from the Zanzibar coast began trading with Buganda in the 1840s and in the 1860s Khartoum-based traders from Egyptian Sudan began to penetrate down the Nile as far as Buganda.

During the reign of Kabaka Mutesa I (1854–84) several developments began which were soon to produce revolutionary changes in Buganda.

a) Islam was introduced through the influence of the Arab traders from the east coast and soon gained many converts.

b) In the early 1870s Khedive Ismail of Egypt tried to expand Egyptian control southwards from the Sudan. From the Egyptian base at Gondokoro on the White Nile first Baker and then Gordon (working for Ismail) interfered greatly in the affairs of the interlacustrine area, establishing some control over the Acholi and Lango peoples in present-day northern Uganda and increasing hostility between Buganda and its old rival Bunyoro.

c) By 1880 the Egyptian threat had disappeared, but it was largely because of this threat that Mutesa welcomed another external influence, Christian missionaries. The first Protestant missionaries from Britain reached Buganda in 1877 and the first Catholics from France in 1879. Both groups rapidly gained converts among the young men working at the kabaka's court.

Thus by the time of Mutesa's death and the accession of Kabaka Mwanga in 1884 the introduction of new ideas had produced new rivalries and conflicts. Mwanga persecuted the Christians in 1885–86 and in 1888 a long civil war began in which Catholics, Protestants, Muslims and traditionalists fought for control of Buganda. Under the leadership of the 'katikiro' (chief minister) Apolo Kagwa, and with British assistance, the Protestant group had established control by the end of the century.

Bunyoro

By the beginning of the nineteenth century, the once very powerful kingdom of Bunyoro had declined greatly: territory had been lost to Buganda and Nkore and in the 1830s Toro reasserted its independence. Bunyoro was governed as a federation of provinces ('saza') each controlled by a chief appointed by the Mukama. During the third quarter of the nineteenth century a very effective Mukama, Kamurasi, began to revive and strengthen Bunyoro by increasing the size of the army, centralising the administration, restoring royal authority and establishing control of the trade routes to the north and east. The next ruler, Kabalega (1879–99), a very able ruler and a great moderniser, continued and extended the work of his predecessor, for example by increasing the size of the well-trained and well-organised standing army to 20,000. By the 1880s Bunyoro probably rivalled Buganda in strength. Despite Egypt's short-lived interference in the late 1870s, Kabalega succeeded in preserving a strong, stable, united

Bunyoro and reconquered many areas (e.g. Toro). In the 1890s Kabalega fought a long guerrilla war against the British until he was captured and exiled in 1899.

Other peoples

Some mention is needed of the important peoples of East Africa who did not live in centralised states. Most of the peoples in the area of present-day Kenya and Tanzania (e.g. the Kikuyu, Kamba, Sukuma and Maasai) lived in various types of segmentary society. Most of these peoples spoke Bantu languages, except in the drier areas where there were Nilotic peoples such as the Maasai and Nandi. Some of these peoples (e.g. the Gogo, Hehe and Sukuma) were divided into many small groups each ruled by a semi-divine chief, often referred to as a Ntemi chief. Others (e.g. the Kikuyu and Kamba) had no chiefs, the main political institution being a complex mixture of councils and age-sets.

One of the most powerful of the peoples of the interior were the Maasai. They were still moving southwards in the first half of the nineteenth century and by 1850 were at the height of their power controlling a huge area from Lake Turkana through the central highlands of Kenya southwards into what is now Tanzania. Their raiding parties affected an even wider area, at times reaching as far as the Indian Ocean and Lake Victoria. The Maasai were a nomadic, pastoral people whose main interests were cattle and war. They were divided into many groups, each organised into age-sets and each with religious leaders known as 'laibons'.

From the 1840s to the 1880s the whole area was disturbed by civil wars between different groups of Maasai, especially between the pastoral Maasai and the agricultural Maasai (known as Kwavi). As a result of these wars whole groups of Maasai (e.g. those of the Uasin Gishu plateau) were destroyed, At the same time the Maasai were weakened by epidemics of cholera, smallpox and cattle plague. Between 1866 and 1890 one laibon, Mbation, united all the pastoral Maasai, but rivalries began again after his death in 1890. By the 1890s the civil wars and epidemics had greatly weakened the Maasai and they were no longer as militarily strong as they had been earlier in the century.

The very numerous Kikuyu people lived in a small, fertile, forested area of the Kenya highlands. They were politically very fragmented living in extended family groups known as 'mbari' linked together by an age-grade system. Throughout the nineteenth century frequent wars were fought against the Maasai.

The most powerful people near the coast were the Shambaa, whose ruler Kimweri (who died in 1860) controlled a large state stretching from the coast to Kilimanjaro. During the second half of the nineteenth century many of the peoples of East Africa were beginning to adjust to rapidly changing circumstances. The pressures of the late nineteenth century (for example the increased use of guns and the spread of insecurity and war) led many peoples to achieve greater strength and unity (for example the Nandi and Luo in what is now western Kenya and the Chagga and Hehe in present-day Tanzania).

9

The Mfecane and its resultant states

Shaka and the rise of the Zulu

The creation of the Zulu state

During the first decades of the nineteenth century a revolution took place among the northern Nguni which affected large areas of southern and eastern Africa. Towards the end of the eighteenth century population pressure produced increasing conflicts between the many small northern Nguni groups in the narrow coastal plain between the northern Drakensberg Mountains and the Indian Ocean. These conflicts enabled larger states than had previously existed to be created by ambitious leaders such as Dingiswayo of the Mthethwa, Zwide of the Ndwandwe, and Sobhuza of the Ngwane. These leaders developed new political and military methods preparing the way for Shaka's creation of the Zulu state.

Shaka was a son of the chief of the small Zulu clan, which was conquered by Dingiswayo soon after 1800. Shaka joined Dingiswayo's army and soon distinguished himself as a great military leader. With Dingiswayo's help Shaka succeeded his father as chief of the Zulu in 1816 and, when Dingiswayo was killed in a war against Zwide in 1818, Shaka became the most powerful leader among the northern Nguni.

In 1819 Shaka defeated Zwide and the Ndwandwe and, supported by a strong army using new types of military organisation and new tactics, soon united the northern Nguni into a highly centralised Zulu state. For a decade Shaka's armies raided far and wide setting off a chain reaction of wars and migrations generally known as the Mfecane (meaning the Time of Troubles). He created a strong, united, military state, but his despotic methods produced opposition. In 1828 Shaka was assassinated by two of his brothers, Dingane and Mhlangana, and Dingane became ruler of the Zulu.

Shaka's achievements

The following were Shaka's main achievements.

a) Army reorganisation. Building upon the reforms of Dingiswayo, Shaka created a revolutionary new type of standing army. His army was composed of age-regiments which joined together men of the same age from all the different groups in the new state and made them totally loyal to Shaka. These age-regiments were well-trained and highly disciplined and were the strongest fighting force the area had known.

b) Military reforms. Shaka also introduced new tactics and new weapons. His soldiers were armed with short stabbing spears which were much more

effective than the traditional throwing spears, and new tactics were used (e.g. the wings or 'horns' of the army surrounding the enemy).
c) Creation of the Zulu state. The many small Nguni chieftaincies were for the first time provided with political and social unity. The Zulu state was strong enough to survive Shaka's death and even today the Zulu possess a strong sense of national identity.
d) Centralisation. The strength and unity of the Zulu state was increased by a high degree of centralisation. All power was in Shaka's hands, the chiefs being closely supervised at his court. The economy was centralised to serve the needs of the army, religious life was transformed to make Shaka the supreme religious leader, and the Zulu language and traditions were adopted by the whole state.

Causes for the rise of the Zulu state

Several factors help to explain the rise of the Zulu state.
a) The pressures produced by a rapidly expanding population made some sort of reorganisation necessary.
b) Influences from the Sotho peoples may have helped to produce change among the northern Nguni.
c) Rivalry to control trade routes (e.g. trade with the Portuguese at Delagoa Bay) may have been a minor contributory factor.
d) Traditional Nguni political and social ideas weakened in the eighteenth century making the Nguni ready to accept great changes.
e) Dingiswayo and Zwide prepared the way by their political and military reforms.
f) Shaka's military reforms and his great abilities as a leader were probably the most important factor.

The Mfecane

Shaka's career and the creation of the Zulu state affected not only the northern Nguni but also all the neighbouring peoples and indirectly influenced the whole of south-eastern Africa. Some peoples were incorporated into the Zulu state, while others moved out of the way of Shaka's armies. These migrations depopulated many areas, spread war and destruction and produced a chain-reaction of further migrations. Some peoples (e.g. the Swazi under Sobhuza and the Sotho under Moshesh) built up nation-states strong enough to resist the Zulu threat, while other groups (e.g. the Ndebele under Mzilikazi and the Gaza under Soshangane) migrated great distances and established new states using Zulu political and military methods. The following were among the main developments of the Mfecane.
a) The northern Nguni, living in the area now called Natal, were either absorbed into the Zulu state or retreated inland across the Drakensberg Mountains or southwards to the southern Nguni area.
b) The Sotho peoples of the interior plains were much disturbed by an influx of groups fleeing from Shaka (e.g. the Hlubi and Tlokwa). Under the very able

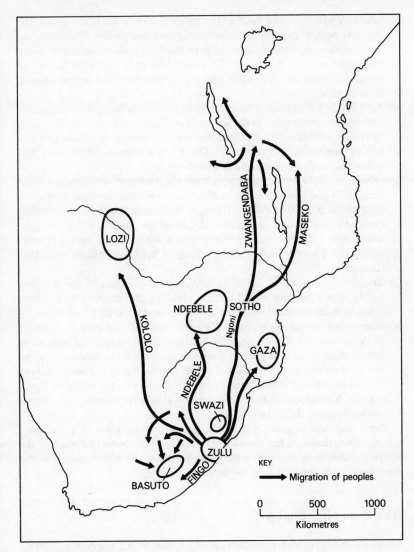

Map 10   The Mfecane

leadership of Moshesh, many moved into the relative security of the Drakensberg Mountains. Moshesh established his capital at Thaba Bosiu and during the 1820s built up a strong Sotho state (which survives today as the independent country of Lesotho).

c) Another example of defensive nation-building is provided by the Swazi. After being defeated by Zwide, Sobhuza moved his Ngwane followers further north. There he and, after 1836, his son Mswati united many Nguni groups into a militarily strong, highly centralised Swazi state.

d) In 1823 Mzilikazi, one of Shaka's generals, fled into the interior with his followers who became known as the Ndebele. For more than a decade the Ndebele caused great destruction throughout present-day Transvaal, increasing their numbers by attaching to themselves the remnants of many conquered peoples. In the late 1830s they were defeated by the Boers and moved further north into what is now Zimbabwe where they created a strong Ndebele state.

e) After Zwide's defeat one of his commanders, Soshangane, moved northwards with his followers known as the Shangane or Gaza. He defeated many groups of Thonga and Shona and created a strong state covering most of the southern half of present-day Mozambique. This Gaza Empire survived until conquered by the Portuguese at the end of the century.

f) Other groups of Zwide's supporters, known as the Ngoni, left Zululand in the early 1820s and spread the effects of the Mfecane three thousand kilometres northwards into eastern Africa. The main Ngoni group, led by Zwangendaba, devastated the Shona area and in 1835 crossed the Zambezi and moved into what is now Tanzania. Another Ngoni group, led by Nqaba, spread destruction along a similar route before settling in the Lake Malawi area. (See Chapter 8.)

g) The Kololo were one of the many Sotho groups displaced by the Mfecane. Led by Sebitwane, they moved northwards along the fringes of the Kalahari desert to the upper Zambezi where they conquered the Lozi. (See Chapter 7.)

h) Many other peoples were affected by the Mfecane: the Pedi in northern Transvaal and the Tswana near the Kalahari desert reorganised themselves into stronger states; the interior plateau area was completely devastated by the activities of warlike groups such as the Ngwane led by Matiwane and the Tlokwa led by MaNtatisi; population pressure among the southern Nguni (e.g. the Xhosa) was increased by the arrival of large numbers of refugees eventually called the Mfengu.

These wars and migrations led to a general redistribution of population. Large fertile areas were left almost empty (e.g. parts of Natal and much of the interior plains) thus facilitating the rapid expansion of white control by the Boer Trekkers in the 1830s and 1840s.

The Zulu after Shaka

Shaka's wars left the Zulu state surrounded by enemies (e.g. the Pondo, Ndebele and Swazi). During Dingane's reign (1828–40) these neighbours were frequently attacked. Dingane lacked Shaka's authority and military skill and there were frequent rebellions by subject chiefs. During the 1820s Shaka had maintained good relations with the first British traders at Port Natal (Durban), but in the 1830s Dingane was faced with increasing pressure from white intruders. In 1835 he made a treaty with Gardiner, leader of the British settlers on the coast, granting part of southern Natal to the British. A greater threat came from the Boer Trekkers led by Piet Retief who wanted to settle in Natal. In early 1838 Dingane ordered the killing of Retief and other Boers. The Boers strengthened themselves under a new leader, Pretorius, and in December 1838 decisively defeated the Zulu at the battle of Blood River. The Boers occupied much of Natal and in 1840

Dingane was deposed and Mpande became ruler of the Zulu with Boer help.

Mpande's long reign was a period of prosperity, stability, peace and consolidation. Through skilful diplomacy, Mpande preserved Zulu unity and maintained peace with his neighbours including the British who had replaced the Boers in Natal in the 1840s. In 1873 Cetshwayo succeeded Mpande and began to revive the strength of the army. By the 1870s the British wished to crush the Zulu in order to prepare the way for a federation of all the white states in southern Africa. In 1879 the British invaded Zululand and were defeated at the battle of Isandhlwana. Later in the year a larger British army captured the Zulu capital at Ulundi and exiled Cetshwayo. This defeat was followed by a period of confusion and in 1887 Zululand was annexed to the British colony of Natal.

Moshesh and the Basuto state

During the disturbances of the Mfecane, Moshesh joined many different groups together into a stable, united Basuto state in the mountainous area between the Orange and Caledon Rivers. He preferred to restore law and order through peaceful policies, but frequently had to fight to preserve his state from enemies such as the Griqua, Tlokwa, Ngwane and Boers. The Basuto nation was not a centralised Zulu-type state, but rather a loose federation of peoples. In 1833 the first missionaries from the Paris Evangelical Missionary Society visited Moshesh and from then on he used the missionaries to help him in his skilful diplomacy with the white communities.

From the 1830s onwards the land-hungry Boer Trekkers were Moshesh's main enemies. Frequent wars were fought (e.g. in 1852, 1858 and 1866) and, although much territory was lost, Basuto independence survived. In 1868 Britain finally agreed to make Basutoland a British protectorate, thus preventing further conflicts with the Boers. In 1870 Moshesh died and in 1880 the Basuto fought the 'War of the Guns' against the British Cape Colony which led to the Basuto state becoming the direct responsibility of the British rather than of the settlers in the Cape.

The Ndebele state

After defeats by the Boers in the 1830s the Ndebele moved northwards from the Transvaal area into what is now Zimbabwe. Mzilikazi established his new capital at Bulawayo and soon conquered the Shona people of the Rozwi confederacy who had already been weakened by the Ngoni. A strong Ndebele state was created covering much of the territory between the Limpopo and Zambezi Rivers. Zulu-type political and military methods were used: the age-regiments were the basis of political power, conquered peoples were fully incorporated and each settlement was headed by a non-royal 'induna'. The Ndebele prospered and in 1868 Mzilikazi was succeeded by his son Lobengula. The first years of Lobengula's reign witnessed a prolonged succession crisis during which Lobengula showed great skill in preserving unity. Even before he had fully established his position as ruler of the Ndebele, Lobengula was faced by growing pressure for mineral concessions by the Boers and the British. Throughout the 1880s he skilfully preserved Ndebele independence, but was eventually forced by increasing European pressure to make some concessions, for example the 1888 Rudd concession to the British South Africa Company.

Cecil Rhodes was determined to extend British authority northwards into Central Africa and in 1893 the Ndebele were conquered by the British South Africa Company. Lobengula died early in 1894.

10

The spread of white control in southern Africa

British rule of the Cape

As part of a European war, the British conquered the Cape (the southernmost part of Africa) from the Dutch in 1806. They decided to retain control of the area because of its strategic position on the sea-route from Europe to Asia. During the first three decades of the nineteenth century the white population of the southern part of Africa trebled from 20,000 to 60,000, as many British settlers joined those of Dutch origin who were known as the Boers.

Most of the Boers were pastoral farmers depending on cattle for which they required huge areas of grazing land. Boer expansion for land and population pressure among the southern Nguni (especially the Xhosa) produced frequent conflicts on the eastern border of the Cape (between 1779 and 1878 there were nine Xhosa wars). Attempts by successive British Governments of the Cape to end these border conflicts had little success: in 1812 the Zuurveld (later called Albany) was annexed and occupied by British settlers; in 1819 an attempt was made to separate the two sides by an empty neutral area; after the very destructive war of 1834–35, an attempt was made to occupy the area between the Fish and Keiskama Rivers which was eventually annexed as British Kaffraria in 1847 after the 'War of the Axe' of 1846–47.

The British made several changes during the first decades of their rule, all of which angered the racialist Boers.

a) A mobile court (known as the Circuit Court) was started in 1811 to hear complaints from Africans against the white settlers.
b) During the 1820s the system of justice was reformed and English law was introduced.
c) The Dutch-based Afrikaans language was gradually replaced by English as the official language.
d) The administration was reformed culminating in the creation of a Legislative Council in 1834.
e) The Fiftieth Ordinance of 1828 gave some civil rights to the African population of the Cape.
f) In 1833 slavery was abolished.

These reforms were strongly supported by the growing number of missionaries, especially members of the London Missionary Society such as Dr John Philip. The missionaries preached equality of all men and were therefore much hated by the Boers.

The Great Trek

Causes

The Great Trek of the late 1830s was largely caused by the growing Boer opposition to British rule. The following were among the most important causes of the Great Trek.

a) As pastoralists the Boers needed a lot of land and were used to moving frequently to new areas.

b) The Mfecane wars of the 1820s had left large areas of the interior underpopulated which led the Boers to believe they could expand into these areas with little opposition.

c) The Boers resented the British Government's attempts to improve African conditions. Boer opposition to the Circuit Court led to the Slagter's Nek rebellion of 1815 as a result of which five Boers were executed. The Fiftieth Ordinance of 1828 and the abolition of slavery in 1833 particularly enraged the strongly racialist Boers.

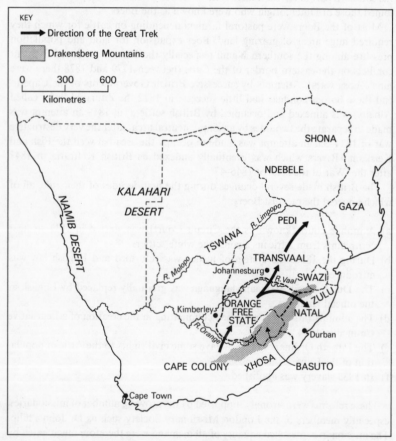

Map 11   The expansion of white control in South Africa

d) Attempts to make the Cape more and more British (e.g. the introduction of English currency, language and law) were resisted by the Boers who wanted to preserve their own Afrikaans language and culture.

e) The Boers were also angered by missionary support for Africans and missionary attempts to free Africans from Boer exploitation.

f) In 1835 the British Governor, d'Urban, tried to annex the area between the Fish and Keiskama Rivers as Queen Adelaide Province, and southern Natal. The British Government, fearing further expensive border conflicts, refused to agree to these annexations. This was the most important immediate cause of the Great Trek for the Boers felt deprived of a chance to occupy rich new lands.

Progress of the Trek

The Great Trek was the migration of about 14,000 Boers from the British Cape into the interior between 1835 and 1845 which led to the creation of the Boer republics of the Orange Free State and the Transvaal (South African Republic). The first groups of trekkers led by Trigardt and van Rensburg left the Cape in 1835. They were ill-prepared and most were eventually killed by disease and by African attacks in the lower Limpopo valley. In 1836 and 1837 much larger groups left the Cape under such leaders as Potgeiter and Maritz. They met with fierce resistence from the Africans, especially from the Ndebele and the Zulu. Well-armed with guns they defeated the Ndebele and forced them to move north and in 1838 defeated the Zulu at Blood River. The defeat of the Zulu led to the creation of the Boer Republic of Natal. The British thought that Boer activities in Natal would increase their own border conflicts and had no wish to see a potentially hostile white power ruling part of the coast. In 1845 the British annexed Natal and most of the Boers moved back into the interior to avoid British rule.

During the 1840s the Boers spread out and occupied a huge area between the Orange and Limpopo Rivers. Several small Boer states were created out of which the Orange Free State and the Transvaal developed. For a short period (1848–54) the British tried to impose their authority over the Boers between the Orange and Vaal Rivers, but by the Sand River Convention of 1852 and the Bloemfontain Convention of 1854 they recognised the full independence of the Transvaal and the Orange Free State. These Boer states had a very simple political organisation with an elected President and an elected Parliament (the 'volksraad'). The Orange Free State was generally more stable than its larger, more densely settled, northern neighbour, the Transvaal.

Results of the Great Trek

The Great Trek was an important turning point in the history of southern Africa with many immediate results and distant repercussions.

a) The Trek brought most of the interior of southern Africa between the Orange and Limpopo Rivers under Boer control. In their new states, the Boers continued their racialist attitudes, out of which the Republic of South Africa's twentieth-century policy of apartheid has developed.

b) Indirectly the Great Trek led to an expansion of the area under British rule. Natal was annexed in 1845 and British Kaffraria in 1847 and conflicts between Boer and African states (e.g. Boer-Basuto wars) involved the British more and more in the affairs of the peoples north of the Orange.

c) This rapid growth in the area under white control led to increasing conflict between white settlers and Africans. The superior weapons of white settlers enabled them in the second half of the nineteenth century to conquer most of the African states of southern Africa (e.g. the Zulu and Ndebele).

d) The creation of independent Boer states resulted in continued rivalry between the British and the Boers and finally a major war at the end of the century.

Thus the Great Trek can be seen to be the origin of many of the problems of the modern Republic of South Africa, such as white rule and apartheid.

The expansion of white rule in the second half of the nineteenth century

The Great Trek led to a vast increase in the area of southern Africa under white rule, a process that continued during the rest of the nineteenth century. This rapid expansion of white, mostly British, rule was generally carried out on the initiative of the white settlers of the Cape rather than by the British Government and was caused by several factors: a desire to control rich agricultural land and mineral deposits, expansion to prevent border warfare with neighbouring African states, and, in the last two decades of the century, imperialism as part of the partition of the whole of Africa. As in the rest of Africa, white conquest was resisted as strongly as possible (e.g. by the Pedi, Xhosa and Zulu). The following were among the main stages of white expansion after 1850.

a) Basutoland. After losing much of its most fertile land to the Boers of the Orange Free State, the Basuto state became a British protectorate in 1868.

b) Griqualand West. This small area at the junction of the Orange and Vaal Rivers became important because of the discovery of large diamond deposits there in 1867. After conflict between the British and the Boers for control of the diamond fields, the British annexed Griqualand West in 1871 and in 1880 it became part of the Cape Colony.

c) Southern Nguni area. The densely populated lands of the southern Nguni between the eastern border of the Cape and Natal (much of which is today known as the Transkei) were gradually conquered by the British and made part of the Cape, for example Fingoland was annexed in 1879, Tembuland in 1884 and Pondoland in 1894.

d) The Pedi. The Pedi of the mountains of the northern Transvaal were conquered in the late 1870s after fierce resistance led by Sekukuni.

e) Namibia. German traders settled at Lüderitz in 1883 and in 1884 Germany annexed a huge area between the Orange River and Angola.

f) Bechuanaland. Fearing a link-up between the Germans in Namibia and the Boers in the Transvaal, the British expanded northwards into the lands of the Tswana people. In 1885 the area between the Orange and Molopo Rivers was annexed as the British Colony of Bechuanaland (in 1895, it became part of the Cape) while a large area north of the Molopo became the British protectorate of Bechuanaland (present-day Botswana).

g) Swaziland. The Swazi state came under the rule of the Transvaal Boers in 1894 but in 1902 was transferred to British rule.

h) Gaza Empire. The Portuguese conquered the Gaza Empire in the 1890s and made it part of their colony of Mozambique.

i) Shona and Ndebele. The conquest of the Shona in 1890 and the Ndebele in 1893 by Cecil Rhodes's British South Africa Company pushed British rule northwards into central Africa.

j) Zululand. In the 1870s the British regarded the Zulu as a threat to their settlers in Natal and as an obstacle for their plans for unity between the white territories. In 1879 the Zulu were defeated, and Zulu strength and unity were destroyed. In 1887 Zululand was annexed to Natal as was Tongaland further north in 1897.

Political and economic developments leading up to the Boer War

During the second half of the nineteenth century, the Cape's system of government changed greatly. In 1853 the Cape was granted representative government (however, only a very few Africans were given the vote) and in 1873 acquired responsible government largely free from British control. By 1870 the white population of the Cape was about 200,000 and this had increased to about half a million by 1900.

Two main themes dominate the history of the white settler states of southern Africa in the second half of the nineteenth century: the discovery of very valuable minerals, and rivalries between the British and the Boers culminating in the Second Anglo-Boer war of 1899–1902 (often referred to simply as the Boer War).

The discovery of diamonds in Griqualand West in 1867 had many important results.

a) The British annexed Griqualand West in 1871.

b) This greatly angered the Boer states and increased the rivalry between the British and the Boers.

c) The purely agricultural economy of the Cape became partly industrialised and stronger with the rapid development of diamond mining.

d) The white population increased greatly (e.g. Kimberley very quickly became the second largest city in southern Africa).

e) By 1900 about 6,000 kilometres of railway had been built in southern Africa.

f) Large numbers of Africans were needed to work in the diamond mines.

g) The de Beers Company, largely owned by Cecil Rhodes, soon gained control of the diamond mines making Rhodes very wealthy and influential.

During the 1870s the British tried to lessen their responsibilities in southern Africa by uniting all the white territories there. Plans for a federation were opposed by the settlers in the Cape who had no wish to be linked with their neighbours who were economically poorer and were threatened by African states such as the Zulu. By 1876 the Transvaal (or South African Republic) was virtually bankrupt as a result of its aggressive policy against African states, its lack of exports, and its poor system of taxation. The Transvaal President, Burgers, asked for British help against the Zulu and in 1877 the British, hoping to further their plans for federation, annexed the Transvaal. The British defeat of the Zulu in 1879 removed the Zulu threat, encouraged the Transvaal Boers to free themselves from British rule and temporarily ended plans for a federation. During the first Anglo-Boer war of 1880–81 the Boers, led by Kruger, defeated the British at the battle of Majuba Hill, and by the Pretoria Convention in 1881 the Transvaal regained almost full independence.

The most influential person in southern Africa in the 1880s was Cecil Rhodes who dominated the de Beers diamond company, Consolidated Goldfields and the British South Africa Company, and in 1890 became Prime Minister of the Cape. He was an imperialist who did everything possible to expand British rule in Africa. He cooperated with Hofmeyer, the Boer leader of the Afrikander Bond, which encouraged good relations between the Boers and British. It was Rhodes's British South Africa Company which was largely responsible for British expansion northwards in the 1890s.

The discovery of gold deposits (the richest in the world) in the Witwatersrand area of the central Transvaal in 1884 completely changed the balance of power in southern Africa. Gold rapidly made the Transvaal economically strong, increased the number of white settlers there (a quarter of a million by 1900), and led to considerable industrialisation (Johannesburg soon becoming the largest city in Africa south of the Sahara). The influx of a large number of mostly British settlers (known as the 'Uitlanders') to work in the gold mines created difficulties. The agricultural Boers and their President, Kruger, were determined to maintain complete Boer control of the Transvaal and so did everything they could to prevent the Uitlanders acquiring citizenship and voting rights.

The question of the voting rights of the Uitlanders led to the Jameson Raid at the very end of 1895. Rhodes encouraged the Uitlanders to rebel and a small British group led by Jameson invaded the Transvaal. The Uitlanders did not rebel, Jameson and his followers were arrested, Rhodes had to resign, and relations between the British and the Boers became worse than ever. As a result of the Jameson Raid, the Transvaal passed harsher legislation against the Uitlanders and all Boers were united in support of Kruger and Transvaal nationalism. In 1897 the imperialist Milner was sent to southern Africa as British High Commissioner and conflict between Milner and Kruger over the problem of the Uitlanders became intense. Both sides began to prepare for war and in October 1899 the second Anglo-Boer war began.

11

Increasing European involvement in Africa, 1800–80

So far, we have been mostly concerned with purely African affairs. In most chapters, however, sections have ended with some form of European take-over, usually in the 1880s or 1890s. During these decades the European powers conquered almost the whole of Africa, a process called the partition of or scramble for Africa. (See Chapter 12.) The partition began very suddenly around 1880, but it is important to realise that it was the culmination of almost a century of increasing European involvement in Africa, some of the most important aspects of which will be considered in this chapter.

In 1880 less than ten per cent of Africa was ruled by Europeans: Algeria, Senegal and South Africa were the only areas where European control extended far inland. During the first three-quarters of the nineteenth century, Britain, France and Portugal were the main European countries with interests in Africa: Portugal was politically and economically very weak; France was very unstable at home and experienced frequent revolutions; and Britain did not wish to involve herself in costly overseas projects. None of the three showed much interest in territorial expansion, but there was considerable European activity in other areas.

During the nineteenth century European travellers visited most parts of Africa giving Europe for the first time some understanding of the geography of the African interior. In the early decades of the century European geographical interest was concentrated on West Africa, especially on the River Niger. From the 1850s interest was focused largely on Central Africa, beginning with Livingstone's trans-continental journey of 1854–56, soon followed by the travels of Burton, Speke, Grant, Baker and Stanley. These travellers were not concerned purely with geography, but were also linked with important aspects of increasing European involvement.

The abolition of the trans-Atlantic slave trade

Slavery and trade in slaves have existed in varying forms in many parts of Africa. In the early nineteenth century slaves were taken from the Western Sudan across the Sahara to North Africa, from large areas of Central Africa to the east coast and to south-west Asia, and from the hinterland of the West coast (from the Senegal River as far south as Angola) across the Atlantic Ocean to North, Central and South America. This last form of slave trade, the trans-Atlantic slave trade, was the most widespread and destructive. During three centuries, tens of millions of Africans were brutally captured and sent across the Atlantic.

The abolition of this evil trade in the first half of the nineteenth century had important results in much of Africa. This trade had been the main reason for European activity in Africa, but paradoxically its abolition strengthened rather than weakened European activity and influence in Africa: abolition had to be enforced; something had to be done with freed slaves; and both trade in other goods and attempts to spread Christianity increased.

Reasons for the abolition

The British, who in the eighteenth century had been very active in the trans-Atlantic slave trade, took the lead in abolishing the trade in the first half of the nineteenth century. The slave trade was made illegal for British subjects in 1807 and slavery was abolished throughout the British Empire in 1833. These measures were, however, only the start of a long and difficult struggle. Two main groups of reasons explain Britain's role in the abolition.

a) Economic reasons. The trans-Atlantic slave trade was vital to eighteenth century Britain largely because of the major role it played in the economy of the sugar-producing British West Indian islands. During the last decades of the eighteenth century these islands became much less important to Britain and at the same time Britain began to industrialise. Both these trends greatly lessened the slave trade's economic importance to Britain. Britain's new industries wanted raw materials (especially palm-oil) from Africa and Britain wanted to sell manufactured goods to Africa. As far as Britain was concerned, the trans-Atlantic slave trade had become economically unnecessary, perhaps even harmful.

b) Humanitarian reasons. The changing economic situation would not have produced such an immediate reaction from the British Government had it not been for humanitarian pressure for abolition. The late eighteenth century witnessed a strong evangelical Christian revival in Britain, one result of which was the setting up of the humanitarian anti-slavery society. Humanitarians like William Wilberforce and Granville Sharpe led a very effective propaganda campaign. In addition, the American and French revolutions in the late eighteenth century helped popularise ideas of equality and justice.

Why abolition took so long

From 1807 onwards the British Government used a variety of methods to try and abolish the slave trade: a naval squadron patrolled the West African coast; diplomatic pressure was used to persuade, bully or bribe other countries to cooperate in abolition; missionary propaganda against the slave trade was intensified; and trade in items other than slaves was encouraged. Some success was achieved: over 1,000 slave ships were captured by the anti-slavery squadron and over 100,000 slaves were released; most other European and American countries had abolished the slave trade by 1830 (e.g. France in 1818 and Brazil in 1825); and Britain went on to persuade most countries to agree to search and equipment treaties which enabled the anti-slave trade squadron to work more effectively. Despite these successes, the slave trade actually increased in the early nineteenth century, and more slaves were seized in the 1830s and 1840s than ever before. The trade was not finally halted until the demand for slaves in the Americas ceased in the 1860s, especially after the abolition of slavery in the USA in 1863.

Several factors help to explain why the abolition of the trans-Atlantic slave trade was such a long, difficult process.

a) Most of the European countries (e.g. Portugal and France) and the American countries (e.g. the USA and Brazil) did not share Britain's desire to abolish the slave trade. They had not yet industrialised and for them the slave trade was still economically valuable. Therefore they were reluctant to enforce anti-slave trade laws forced on them by the British.

b) During the early nineteenth century there was an increased demand for slaves to work in the plantations of Cuba and Brazil and to expand the cotton-growing area in the south of the USA.

c) Many nations distrusted Britain's anti-slave trade activities and regarded them as threats to their independence (e.g. the USA consistently refused to sign search and equipment treaties).

d) The small British squadron had a huge area of ocean and over 6,000 kilometres of coastline to patrol. Much of the coast provided ideal conditions for slavers to continue their trade undetected (e.g. in the creeks of the Niger Delta).

e) Many coastal African leaders benefited from the slave trade and so wished to continue it as long as possible. Abolition was supported only by those who had developed a profitable alternative to the slave trade (e.g. trade in palm-oil), such as the Efik of Calabar. Many Africans justifiably regarded British anti-slave trade activities as attempts to interfere in local politics and expand British control.

The growth of legitimate trade

One reason why the abolition of the trans-Atlantic slave trade did not lead to a decrease in European activity in Africa was the fact that during the first half of the nineteenth century trade in goods other than slaves, known as legitimate trade, expanded. Africa's exports had for long been varied and included timber, hides, gum and gold. During the early nineteenth century, trade in palm-oil from West Africa and ivory from East Africa increased greatly and eventually replaced slaves as the major trading article. Between 1820 and 1850 West Africa's annual export of palm-oil (needed as a lubricant in Europe's growing industries) rose from 1,000 to 30,000 tonnes, and during the period 1780–1830 the price of ivory increased ten times.

In most areas Britain took the lead in developing legitimate trade because Britain was the first to industrialise and was eager for legitimate trade as an alternative to slave trade. European travellers and missionaries emphasised, and often exaggerated, the prospects of trade with the interior and, from the middle of the century onwards, more and more of the interior was drawn into a wider trading economy. By the 1870s European trading companies were beginning to penetrate inland (e.g. along the Senegal and Niger Rivers) and competiton between European traders and between European traders and African middlemen was becoming more intense. This expansion of European economic activity in Africa in many ways prepared the way for eventual European conquest, but it must be remembered that export trade was not Africa's only trade: much internal trade (e.g. the kola nut trade from the Asante area to the savannah) continued and increased.

Christian missionaries

Closely linked with the abolition of the slave trade and the development of legitimate trade was the spread of Christian missionary work in Africa.

The beginnings of Christian missionary work

Portuguese attempts to introduce Christianity into various parts of Africa in the sixteenth century achieved little. The first modern missionary societies date from the late eighteenth and early nineteenth centuries and, like the anti-slave trade society, they were by-products of the evangelical revival. Among the earliest missionary societies founded in Britain were the Baptist Missionary Society (founded 1792), the London Missionary Society (1795) and the Church Missionary Society (1799). About the same time similar Protestant missions were started in the USA, the German states and Switzerland. Among the earliest Catholic missionary societies were the Society for the Propogation of the Faith (1822) and the Holy Ghost Fathers (1837). The following were among the earliest areas of missionary activity.

a) South Africa. The earliest missionary work was in the second half of the eighteenth century (e.g. Van Der Kemp who worked with the Khoikhoi and Xhosa). In the early nineteenth century the number of missionaries, mostly English (e.g. Dr John Philip of the London Missionary Society), increased greatly.

b) West Africa. The Church Missionary Society began work in Sierra Leone in 1806 and in Abeokuta in 1844. The Methodists started working in Sierra Leone in 1811, among the Fante in 1833 and in Abeokuta in 1844, while the Presbyterians began work in Calabar in 1844. Many freed slaves, Christianised in Sierra Leone, returned to their homelands and played a major part in the early spread of Christianity.

c) East Africa. In 1844 Ludwig Krapf began work for the Church Missionary Society at Rabai near Mombasa. He was soon joined by two others, Rebman and Erhardt, but they met with little initial success. Even before this the London Missionary Society had achieved much in the central highlands of Madagascar, and claimed over 4,000 pupils in their schools by 1835.

Developments after 1850

Until the middle of the nineteenth century, missionary activity did not extend far inland. The rapid expansion of missionary work into the interior of central Africa was largely the result of the journeys of the missionary-traveller Livingstone. He saw the destruction caused by the Arab-Swahili slave trade and feared the spread of Islam. At about the same time as Livingstone was urging Protestants to expand into the interior, Cardinal Lavigerie was using similar arguments to encourage Catholic missionary expansion. The decade following Livingstone's death in 1873 was a period of rapid missionary advance into the interior: Anglicans began work in Buganda in 1877 and Catholics in 1878; Scottish Presbyterian missions were established near Lake Malawi (Livingstonia, 1875) and the Universities' Mission to Central Africa began work at Masasi, in what is now southern Tanzania, in 1876.

Similar missionary expansion took place in South and West Africa. In South Africa missionaries were particularly active among the Sotho and Tswana and began to move north along the 'missionary road'. In West Africa mission work was intensified in areas such as Yorubaland and the Niger Delta.

One major concern of missionaries everywhere was the abolition of the slave trade and the care of freed slaves. Homes for freed slaves were established by the Holy Ghost Fathers at Bagamoyo in 1868 and by the Church Missionary Society at Freretown in 1875, and, on a larger scale, Sierra Leone provides the best example of missionary work among freed slaves.

Some missionaries hoped to convert from the top and concentrated their work at the courts of powerful rulers such as Mutesa of Buganda and Lewanika of the Lozi. Nowhere were missionaries welcomed for religious reasons: societies either opposed them or initially welcomed them for non-religious reasons. The Egba of Abeokuta at first welcomed missionaries in order to gain advantage in the Yoruba civil wars and protection against Dahomey: when missionaries began to get too powerful, the Egba drove them out, the 'Ifole' of 1867. Only in a few areas with special conditions (for example Sierra Leone and Buganda) was there any large-scale conversion before the establishment of colonial rule.

The effects of Christian missionary work

Although the full impact of Christian missionaries was not felt until the twentieth century, several effects of their work began to be felt in the second half of the nineteenth century in many parts of Africa.

a) Religious effects. Christian missionaries did everything possible to weaken traditional religion, and in some areas Christianity soon became the religion of an influential minority.

b) Social effects. Missionaries helped to abolish slavery and the slave trade. They also persuaded rulers to abolish traditional customs which they did not approve of (e.g. the Calabar kings were persuaded to ban human sacrifice). Also closely linked with Christian missionaries was the introduction and gradual spread of European-style education. At first mission education was largely primary, but by the end of the nineteenth century there were a few secondary and technical mission schools in the coastal areas of West Africa and in South Africa.

c) Political effects. In many areas (e.g. the Niger Delta and Buganda) the presence of missionaries increased divisions within society, thus lessening the ability to resist colonial attack later in the century. The activities of European missionaries involved European governments more and more in African affairs and in many ways paved the way for the establishment of colonial rule, (e.g. British rule in such areas as Malawi, Buganda and Yorubaland was partly the result of British missionary work).

d) Other effects. Missionaries were also influential in other areas, such as:
- linguistics. Missionaries took the lead in the study of African languages in order to translate the Bible into the vernacular.
- building. Missionaries introduced new styles of architecture and new methods of building.
- printing. Missionaries were often involved in the earliest printing and the first newspapers.
- medicine. Some missionaries specialised in health problems and did pioneering medical work.

Sierra Leone and Liberia

Mention needs to be made of Sierra Leone and Liberia whose foundation and history were closely linked with the abolition of the trans-Atlantic slave trade, the growth of legitimate trade and with Christian missions.

Sierra Leone

Groups of freed slaves from Britain, Nova Scotia and Jamaica formed a settlement at Freetown in the last years of the eighteenth century. This project was organised by Granville Sharpe and the Sierra Leone Company, an offshoot of the anti-slave trade society. These first settlers had a lot of problems because of disease, hostility from the local Temne people and ignorance of tropical agriculture. In just over a decade half the original 3,000 settlers died. The settlement became too expensive for the Sierra Leone Company to run and in 1807 the British Government took over Sierra Leone as Britain's first West African colony. Freetown became the base for the British anti-slave trade squadron and it was there that the slaves from ships seized by the squadron were freed. About 70,000 of these freed slaves, known as the recaptives, were freed in Sierra Leone during the first half of the nineteenth century.

British missionaries and the British colonial government (especially Charles Macarthy Governor of Sierra Leone from 1814 to 1824) worked hard to convert the recaptives to Christianity and give them a European-style education. So successful were they that in 1861 the Church Missionary Society withdrew its missionaries, leaving complete control of the church to Sierra Leoneans, and also by the 1860s a higher proportion of children were attending school in Sierra Leone than in Britain. By the middle of the nineteenth century the recaptives had intermarried and merged with the original negro settlers to produce a distinctive group of people known as the Creoles, with their own language and culture. For the next half-century these educated, Christian Creoles had a very great influence all along the West African coast in the following matters.

a) Education. Many primary and secondary schools were established so that the Creoles could obtain a high standard of education. In 1827 Fourah Bay College was started to train African clergy and in 1876 it became a degree-awarding college of the University of Durham. Many Creoles qualified in professions such as law and medicine, important books were written and printed,

and Freetown became the intellectual centre of coastal West Africa.
b) Religion. From 1861 the Sierra Leonean church was completely staffed and controlled by Creoles. Many recaptives returned to their original homes (e.g. Abeokuta), taking Christianity with them.
c) Trade. Creoles dominated and expanded trade all along the West African coast from Cameroon to Senegal.
d) Government. From 1863 there were Creole members of the Sierra Leone Legislative and Executive Councils and by the 1870s over half the senior civil service positions were held by Creoles. When the British expanded their control over West Africa later in the century, Creoles were appointed to senior civil service positions throughout British West Africa.

From the late 1890s Creole influence began to decline. By then British attitudes were far more racialist, and the British governor of Sierra Leone, Cardew, used the 1898 war against the Temne and Mende as an excuse for discriminating against the Creoles.

Liberia

Liberia was similar to Sierra Leone in origin and influence. The American Colonisation Society sent the first free slaves to Cape Mesurado in 1821, and this first settlement eventually grew into the city of Monrovia. Many groups of American blacks joined the first settlers and, although the settlers experienced many difficulties similar to those of the first Sierra Leoneans, rapid political progress was made. In 1847 the independent Republic of Liberia was established with an American style constitution.

During the second half of the nineteenth century Liberia faced many problems such as political disunity, economic weakness and conflict between the Americo-Liberians and the Africans. Despite this, Liberia survived the partition as an independent nation and produced many men of great influence throughout West Africa (e.g. the writer E. W. Blyden).

Immediate background to the partition

While the slave trade remained Europe's main interest in Africa, there was little direct European social and political impact. During the nineteenth century, however, the abolition of the slave trade, the growth of legitimate trade, and Christian missionary activity all greatly increased European interference in the affairs of African peoples.

During the period 1850–80 European activity increased in many parts of Africa.
a) European influence increased in Morocco, Tunisia and Egypt.
b) The French consolidated their control over Algeria.
c) The French, led by Faidherbe, expanded inland along the Senegal River.
d) The British expanded their interests in West Africa with the annexation of Lagos in 1861, the creation of the Gold Coast Colony in 1874 and greater interference in the Niger Delta states.
e) The area under white control in South Africa was much enlarged.
f) The British increasingly interferred in the affairs of Zanzibar and of the East African coast.

g) European missionaries began working in parts of the interior.

Expansion of European control in the 1870s was still slow and gradual with little indication of the sudden expansion which was to occur in the 1880s. Only in Algeria, Senegal and South Africa did Europeans rule more than small coastal trading stations. European governments were, however, coming under increasing pressure from various groups (traders, missionaries, adventurers, politicians) to expand the area of Africa under their control.

12

The partition of Africa

Between 1880 and 1905 European powers (especially Britain, France, Germany, Portugal, Belgium and Italy) moved into most of Africa except Ethiopia and Liberia. This sudden and rapid involvement is usually called the partition of Africa. The most important aspects of this topic are the causes for the partition, the general pattern of partition and African resistance to conquest and why this resistance failed.

Causes of the partition

By the 1880s Europe was better able to consider overseas expansion than ever before. The discovery of quinine to prevent malaria had greatly improved the health of Europeans in tropical areas and during the nineteenth century European governmental and bureaucratic methods had been rapidly developed, making the effective administration of large, distant empires possible. Even more significant was the development of simpler, cheaper, and more deadly weapons (e.g. the first machine guns were invented in the 1860s and brought into general use in the 1880s). Such factors as these made the partition possible, but did not cause it. The partition was caused by a complex mixture of long-term and immediate factors, mostly European rather than African. There is much dispute about the relative importance of the various factors, but it is generally agreed that long-term economic and political changes in Europe were of major importance and that a series of events in the years 1878–85 sparked off the partition.

Long-term causes

a) Economic.
-   By the last decades of the nineteenth century other European countries (e.g. Germany, Belgium and France) were beginning to catch Britain up in industrialisation. This produced greater competition for the raw materials (cash crops and minerals) of Africa and for markets in which to sell surplus manufactured goods. In fact Africa never became of great trading importance to Europe (e.g. trade with Africa remained about five per cent of Britain's overseas trade), but in the 1880s many had an exaggerated idea of the economic potential of Africa based on the accounts of travellers such as Stanley in the Congo and Barth in the Western Sudan.
-   This growing competition for raw materials and markets and the economic depression of the 1880s encouraged European traders, previously active only

71

on the coasts of Africa, to push into the interior. This produced increasing conflict with African middlemen and so traders put more and more pressure on their home governments to establish colonies so that they could trade safely and without competition.

- Linked with this was the growing trend away from free trade towards protectionist policies (e.g. in France). The European powers did not wish to be excluded from the trade of areas of Africa by potentially protectionist rivals.
- Some have argued that the desire to find places in which to invest surplus capital was a major cause of the partition. However, very little European capital was ever invested in Africa (except in Egypt and South Africa) and only in those two areas were opportunities for investment and the protection of existing investments major factors.
- The discovery in South Africa of the Kimberley diamond fields in the 1860s and the Rand gold fields in the 1880s made the Europeans aware of the possibility of finding mineral wealth in other parts of Africa.

b) Political.

- Germany's unification and emergence as a major world power (completed by the defeat of France in the Franco-Prussian war of 1870–71) greatly changed the relationship between the powers of Europe. The period after 1871 is sometimes called the period of 'armed peace': the rise of Germany had upset the European balance of power and produced great rivalry and instability in international affairs. There was no longer any room for the great powers to expand in Europe and so competitive were they that, if any of them gained territory outside Europe, the others would seek compensatory extensions so as not to allow any to gain an advantage.
- Political factors encouraging partition were especially strong in France. France had been humiliatingly defeated by Germany in 1871 and had lost two of her provinces. From then on the French army was eager to regain prestige by overseas conquest. Some French politicians also argued in favour of the need for a large overseas empire to supply the manpower necessary in a future war of revenge against Germany. These motives help to explain why France conquered huge areas of little or no economic value (e.g. most of the Sahara desert).
- Another political factor, especially important to the British, was the protection of areas of strategic importance. The security of the sea-routes to India around the Cape and through the Suez Canal were major concerns of Britain. The need to control these routes concentrated Britain's attention on Egypt and South Africa and this helps explain why British expansion was largely in southern and eastern Africa and along the Nile.
- Political considerations also help to explain Germany's role in the partition. Bismarck, the German Chancellor, wanted African colonies to use as bargaining counters in his European diplomacy.

c) Other.

- For various reasons racialist feelings of white superiority became popular in Europe towards the end of the nineteenth century. Mistaken ideas about the white race's divine mission to rule provided a theoretical justification for the partition.
- Another important psychological cause for the partition was European

nationalism. The European powers were trying to prove their greatness and one way of doing this was to rule a large empire. This factor is particularly important in explaining the creation of an Italian empire in northern and north-eastern Africa.

- Small groups of individuals were often vital in persuading European governments to expand in Africa. In addition to traders like Sir George Taubman Goldie on the Niger and Sir William MacKinnon in East Africa, missionaries were sometimes of great importance (e.g. in producing British rule in Botswana, Malawi and Buganda), as were adventurer-imperialists such as Cecil Rhodes in South and Central Africa, Karl Peters in East Africa and King Leopold II of Belgium in the Congo area.

Immediate causes

As late as 1880, European governments had little interest in territorial expansion in Africa, but so great was the change in attitude in the early 1880s that at the end of 1884 the European powers held a conference at Berlin to lay down the rules for the partition, which by then was well under way, and to prevent the scramble for Africa producing conflicts between them. The diplomacy of the period 1878–85, which provides both the immediate causes and the first stages of the partition, was extremely complex, but from among the mass of interrelated events the following may be selected as the most important immediate causes of the partition.

a) In the late 1870s the French, eager for prestige and military victory of any kind, began the conquest of the Western Sudan from their base in the Senegal valley.

b) Also during the late 1870s King Leopold II of Belgium, who wanted a personal empire in Africa, began to extend his activities in the Congo basin.

c) In the early 1880s relations between the British and the Boer Transvaal Republic were very hostile (e.g. the Boer defeat of the British at Majuba Hill in 1881). This hostility, intensified by the discovery of gold in the Transvaal, accelerated British expansion in South Africa.

d) Perhaps the most important immediate cause of the partition was the British occupation of Egypt in 1882. Britain wanted to protect her investments in Egypt and to control the vital Suez Canal route to India. The British occupation of strategically-important Egypt alarmed the other European powers, especially the French.

e) Largely in reaction to the British occupation of Egypt, the French in 1882 established claims over much of the north bank of the River Congo – the Makoko treaties. This sudden French claim in the Congo basin alarmed the Germans, the Portuguese, the British and King Leopold. It was largely the Congo question that led to the Berlin Conference of 1884–85.

f) The speed of European expansion in Africa was further increased by the claim of Germany, previously not interested in colonial expansion, to four parts of Africa (Togo, Cameroon, Namibia and Tanganyika) in 1884.

The pattern of the partition

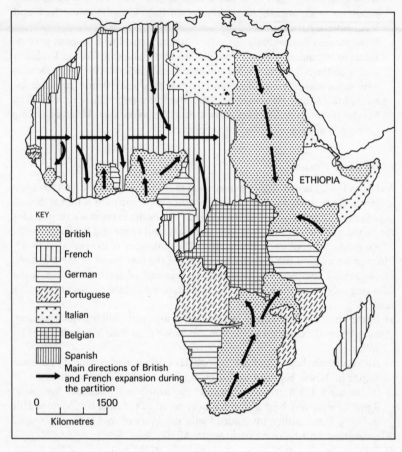

Map 12   Africa after the partition, 1914

Each of the major colonial powers had certain areas of special interest and developed certain main directions of expansion.

a) Britain. During most of the nineteenth century the British Government was strongly opposed to the establishment of colonies in Africa, considering them a financial burden (e.g. in 1865 a parliamentary report recommended that Britain should abandon all her interests in West Africa except Freetown). British opposition to colonial expansion continued well into the 1880s. In fact by 1885 the sudden acquisitions by France, Germany and Belgium had seized many coastlines where Britain had previously been active. During the period 1885–91, when Lord Salisbury was Prime Minister, Britain accepted the need for colonial expansion and began to reassert herself after having joined the scramble rather late. Britain's main direction of expansion was north-south across Africa between Egypt and South Africa. Britain's concern for Egypt led her into the Nile valley areas of the Sudan and Uganda, and from South Africa, largely through the initiative of Cecil Rhodes, Britain expanded northwards to Botswana and Central Africa. West Africa was of less strategic importance to Britain and there expansion was limited to areas of earlier trader activity (e.g. the Niger area and Ghana) or missionary activity (e.g. Yorubaland).

b) France. Throughout the nineteenth century France was politically unstable with frequent changes of government and varying attitudes to colonial expansion. This allowed the Ministry of the Marine, which was responsible for the colonies, and the Army great freedom of action. The French conquest of the Western Sudan (the present-day countries of Senegal, Mali, Upper Volta, Mauritania and Niger) and the interior of French Equatorial Africa (Chad and the Central African Republic) was almost entirely a military affair. In the French coastal colonies (e.g. Ivory Coast, Dahomey and Gabon) French expansion was prepared for by traders. By the middle of the 1880s the French had developed an overall plan for expansion. They wanted to expand eastwards across the Western Sudan to Lake Chad and on to their small Red Sea colony (Djibouti) at the same time linking up northwards with their long-established colony in Algeria and southwards with Gabon and French Congo. The French achieved these very ambitious aims except in the Nile valley where their east-west moves were thwarted by British north-south expansion (the Fashoda incident of 1898). In addition the French expanded their North African empire (just across the Mediterranean from France) by adding Tunisia and most of Morocco to Algeria, and they also took the large Indian Ocean island of Madagascar.

c) Germany. Germany's colonial aims were more limited than those of Britain and France. Germany's activities in Africa in the 1880s were decided largely by Bismarck in order to further his European diplomatic objectives. The four German colonies (Togo, Cameroon, Namibia and Tanganyika) were established in areas where German traders were already present. German expansion north-east from Namibia and south-west from Tanganyika was blocked by Cecil Rhodes's expansion northwards from South Africa on behalf of the British.

d) Portugal. Portugal had held small coastal African colonies since the late fifteenth century. In the nineteenth century Portugal was one of the poorest and weakest European countries. She succeeded in claiming large hinterlands to her Angola and Mozambique coastal enclaves, but British expansion northwards from South Africa prevented her joining them across Africa from east to west.

e) Others. Other European powers involved in the partition were Belgium, Italy and Spain. Belgium's huge colony in the Congo basin (present-day Zaïre) was entirely the creation of King Leopold II who persuaded the other European powers to accept the formation of the Congo Free State, a sort of personal empire, at the Berlin Conference. Italy's ambitions were restricted to north-eastern Africa where she took Somalia, Eritrea and later Libya, but was defeated by Ethiopia. Spain's interests were small and largely restricted to the north-western coast.

During the 1880s the partition was largely a partition on paper, European powers arbitrarily fixing boundaries with no reference to the land and peoples of Africa. By the early 1890s the broad pattern of the partition had been largely settled: what remained was the actual conquest, the finalisation of boundaries and the establishment of effective administration. The 1890s were the main decade of conquest, although in many areas resistance was so strong that fighting continued well into the twentieth century: actual conquest was often as many as twenty years after the initial establishment of claims. Often trading companies were used as a means of trying to establish control cheaply, for example the Royal Niger Company, the British South Africa Company and the German East Africa Company. The task of conquest and administration soon proved too expensive for most companies and the colonial governments had to take over. The various stages of the partition were complex and interconnected: many of the main events during the partition are mentioned in other chapters.

Resistance to European Conquest

The extent of resistance

Most of what has already been said has been concerned more with the conquerors than the conquered. Historians have often emphasised the European rather than the African aspects of the partition and have underestimated the strength of African resistance to European conquest. African reactions varied: some peoples were too internally divided to offer much resistance, some (e.g. the Baganda and the Lozi) sought to gain benefit through cooperation with the Europeans, but most defended their independence in every possible way.

Even with their enormous weapon superiority it was not easy for the European powers to divide up Africa. It was a long, difficult process taking over a quarter of a century and costing much more than European governments had expected. By the early 1890s European forces were engaged in major conflicts in every part of Africa (e.g. in the Congo, Tanganyika, Madagascar, Ethiopia, Asante and the Western Sudan). Only Ethiopia survived the partition by inflicting a major defeat on the Europeans (the battle of Adowa 1896), but many peoples avoided effective conquest until well into the twentieth century (e.g. the Baoule of the southern Ivory Coast, the peoples of the Jos Plateau of central Nigeria, the Cokwe of Angola and the Yao of Mozambique).

Most large states with well-developed armies offered resistance (e.g. the Tokolor Empire, the Sokoto Caliphate, Mahdist Sudan, the Ndebele and the Zulu). Even more difficult to conquer were those living in segmentary societies (e.g. the Igbo and Tiv) who had to be gradually brought under control village by village. In many areas conquest was not final: as soon as the impact of colonial rule began to be felt, the people rebelled (e.g. the Shona-Ndebele rebellion of 1896–97 in present-day Zimbabwe, the Maji-Maji rebellion of 1905–07 in Tanganyika and the rebellions in many parts of the French Western Sudan during the First World War, 1914–18).

Examples of resistance

So widespread and determined was African resistance to European conquest that space will not permit a full account. A few examples must be sufficient to show the magnitude of their resistance:

a) Samori Toure. Samori Toure, the Mandinka ruler (see Chapter 5), provides one of the best examples of effective resistance to European occupation. He built up a well-trained and well-equipped standing army to defend the empire he had created in the 1860s and 1870s in what is now northern Guinea and Ivory Coast. In the early 1880s he first came into conflict with the French expanding from Senegal towards the Niger. Despite the conquest of his first empire by the French in 1891, he continued fighting further east until he was finally captured in 1898. Throughout this long war Samori made the best possible use of his small, skilled army. He avoided large battles against the French, but instead made use of guerrilla tactics. During his retreat eastwards in the early 1890s, 'scorched earth' tactics were used to delay the French advance.

b) Arab-Swahili resistance. In East and Central Africa some of the most determined resistance to European conquest came from the Swahili of the coast and the Arab traders around Lakes Malawi and Tanganyika and in the eastern Congo. On the Tanganyika coast Abushiri of Pangani and Bwana Heri of Saadani led rebellions against the Germans in 1888–89. Over a large area of the interior Swahili and Arab traders fought against the forces of Germany, Britain and Leopold's Free State. The Free State forces had a long struggle in the 1890s to defeat Arabs such as Tippu Tip's son, Sef, in the eastern Congo. Around Lake Malawi the British fought for over a decade against Arabs such as Mlozi of Karonga who was finally defeated by the British in 1895.

c) The Tiv. The Tiv of central Nigeria provide a good example of strong resistance from a people living in a segmentary society. The British first came into conflict with the Tiv in 1900 when the Tiv attacked a British group trying to erect a telegraph line across their country. Twice again in 1901 and 1906 the British sent military forces against the Tiv. After 1906 the British gradually expanded the area of Tivland under their control avoiding military conflict wherever possible.

d) The Herero and Nama. The Bantu Herero and the Khoikhoi Nama are two of the largest groups in Namibia. This largely desert and semi-desert country became a German colony in 1884 and by the mid 1890s through force and skilful diplomacy the Germans had gained the cooperation of Hendrik Witbooi, the Nama leader, and Samuel Maherero, the Herero leader. In 1904, however, both groups rose against the Germans. The Herero rebellion in January to August 1904 was brutally crushed by General von Trotha with about three-quarters of the Herero being killed. Despite this treatment of the Herero, the Nama rebelled later in 1904 and continued fighting using guerrilla tactics until 1907.

e) The Senussiya. The Muslim Senussiya brotherhood in the deserts of Libya fiercely resisted Italian conquest. The Italian take-over of the Turkish provinces of Tripolitania and Cyrenaica in 1911–12 made the Senussiy sheikhs political and nationalist, as well as religious, leaders. Led by Sayyid Ahmad until 1918, and then by Sayyid Idris, the Senussiya kept an Italian army of 20,000 occupied right up until the 1930s.

Why the Europeans were successful

How then were the Europeans able, despite this strong resistance, to seize virtually the whole of Africa so rapidly?

a) The first and perhaps most important reason was the greatly superior weapons available to the Europeans. The industrial revolution had produced a great advance in weapon technology, culminating in the invention of the Maxim and Gatling guns, early types of machine-gun, in the 1860s. The few guns possessed by African states were old and of little use against the Europeans' ever-more deadly weapons. Most African leaders relied on traditional weapons (e.g. spears and bows and arrows).

b) The traditional tactics used by African armies (e.g. massed cavalry, walled cities) were unsuited to the new kind of enemy with modern weapons. African armies varied greatly in size, organisation and equipment, but all had been developed to deal with African enemies. Most African peoples had to continue dealing with African conflicts during the partition and so could not risk completely reorganising their armies and tactics to suit the needs of defence against the European threat. Only a few leaders (e.g. Samori Toure and Mkwawa of the Hehe) adopted more suitable and more effective guerrilla tactics.

c) The peoples and states of Africa were reluctant to ally against the Europeans. Deep-seated rivalries prevented them presenting a united front and enabled the Europeans to conquer them one by one. In some cases there was cooperation with the Europeans in order to gain advantage over African rivals (e.g. Fante support for the British against Asante, Baganda support for the British against Bunyoro).

d) Moreover most African peoples were internally divided. Succession disputes led to rival claimants to the throne and many of the larger states were the creations of nineteenth century upheavals (e.g. the jihads and the Mfecane) and were still unstable, containing discontented subject groups eager to reassert their independence.

e) Much of Africa lacked natural barriers, and open savannah land facilitated the rapid movement of large armies. Where natural barriers did exist (e.g. the mountains of Ethiopia, the forests of the Congo and the Sahara desert) conquest was most difficult and delayed.

f) Most African states were primarily agricultural with low population density and lacked the resources for prolonged warfare.

Effects of the partition

The partition of Africa ranks together with the jihads and the Mfecane as one of the most important developments of the nineteenth century. Here it is only necessary to give a very brief outline of the effects of the partition, since virtually everything in the following chapters on colonial rule is directly or indirectly the result of the partition. Basically the partition greatly speeded up the pace of change by establishing colonial rule, which had many effects.

a) Political. The partition led to the loss of independence. No longer did Africans rule Africans: whether African rulers were destroyed during the partition or retained to assist in colonial rule, the political structure had fundamentally changed, the final decisions and control coming from the European colonial authorities. The partition created the modern map of Africa. A few states (e.g. Tunisia, Rwanda, Lesotho) survived the partition with only slight boundary changes, but most states and peoples were joined into larger units which have now emerged as independent African countries.

b) Economic. The partition led to European economic exploitation: railways were built and cash crop production was encouraged.

c) Social. The partition undermined traditional society and religion, and facilitated the spread of Islam, Christianity and education. Many lives were lost and much suffering was caused by the wars during and after the partition.

13

Colonial rule: early stages and main types

It is difficult to decide how to divide up and organise the information on colonial rule in twentieth century Africa. Chapters 16–20 will describe the main developments during the colonial period on a regional basis since many examination syllabuses use regional divisions. This chapter, and the next two, will indicate some of the important aspects of colonial rule affecting more of Africa than merely one region, thus avoiding repetition in the regional chapters.

General points

A few introductory points must be clearly understood.
a) Every part of Africa, except Liberia, experienced European colonial rule at some stage during the twentieth century.
b) European colonial rule was established over most of Africa during the partition in the last two decades of the nineteenth century and the first decade of the twentieth century. During the last quarter-century colonial rule has been ended almost everywhere in Africa. Therefore, except for the generally small, old-established coastal colonies, colonial rule lasted for only between fifty and seventy years, and where firm control was delayed by resistance the period of effective colonial rule was even shorter.
c) The general importance of colonial rule should not be exaggerated. It was certainly not the cause of all twentieth-century developments. In many parts of Africa important changes (e.g. the introduction of cash crops) had begun before colonial rule. None of the colonial powers made any real attempt to modernise and develop their African colonies until after the Second World War.
d) In most of tropical Africa the period of colonial rule can be divided into three main sections: the establishment of colonial rule 1890–1920 (conquest, pacification and the beginnings of administration); full colonial rule 1920–45 (colonial rule fully established and not yet much questioned); and rapid decolonisation 1945–65 (when almost all colonial territories gained their independence).
e) All colonial governments had certain fundamental aims in common, especially financial self-sufficiency for their colonies and the creation and preservation of peace.
f) Central government, at least until the last years of colonial rule, was completely controlled by Europeans. Local government was sometimes direct (where European officials were used at every level as much as possible) and

sometimes indirect (where more use was made of traditional African authorities).

g) Developments in Algeria and South Africa were unique because they were old-established, settler-dominated colonies. Egypt, Tunisia and Morocco were also ruled rather differently from the rest of Africa as they were protectorates. Apart from these special cases colonial rule in the rest of Africa (mostly tropical Africa) was in many ways similar. One important distinction was that between colonies of settlement in the largely highland south and east of Africa (e.g. Angola, Zimbabwe and Kenya) and colonies of exploitation in the more lowland north and west (e.g. Gabon, Nigeria and Senegal).

Early stages

During the first two decades of the twentieth century the main activities of the colonial powers were completing the conquest, finalising boundaries, suppressing rebellions and creating the beginnings of government. There was generally a great shortage of European officers (both civilian and military), and resistance was determined, so, in many areas, firm control was not established until the second or third decade of the century (e.g. the Portuguese were not in full control of Angola until 1915, Mozambique until the 1920s and Guinea-Bissau until the 1930s). This was a period of great devastation in many parts of Africa: it has been estimated that the population of Central Africa was halved between 1880 and 1930 as a result of the Arab slave trade, European conquest, disease, famine and rebellion.

The earliest forms of colonial government were imposed with little or no knowledge of the societies involved and at a time when the Europeans were still largely concerned with completing the conquest. Not surprisingly, an enormous variety of methods of colonial rule were introduced, much depending on the ideas of the individual on the spot. It was not until the 1920s that reasonably clear, planned ideas and methods of rule began to emerge. In the early years the difficulty of financing a colony did much to determine its system of government and prevented development.

Even after they had been brutally conquered, most Africans were far from resigned to foreign domination and continued to resist. This resistance took many forms (e.g. the growth of independent Christian churches, migration and armed rebellion), and provides a link between the initial opposition to European conquest during the partition and the rise of nationalism and the struggle for independence. During the early years of the twentieth century many Europeans were so shocked by the cruelty of colonial rule (e.g. the exploitation of rubber in the Congo and German brutality in Namibia) that they advocated reform. Before much could be achieved, the First World War (1914–18) intervened and affected Africa in many ways.

The First World War

The First World War was basically a European war in which most of the colonial powers (France, Britain, Belgium, and later Italy) fought against Germany. It brought Africa more into world affairs, emphasised the strategic and economic importance of Africa and marked an important turning-point in the development of colonial rule. The following were among the most important effects of the First World War on Africa.

a) Fighting. Actual fighting in Africa was confined to the four German colonies. The British and French and their allies quickly seized control of Togo and Namibia, but the conquest of Cameroon took two years and fighting continued throughout the war in Tanganyika causing much bloodshed, suffering and destruction.

b) Recruitment. Most of the soldiers in all these campaigns were Africans, and Africans were also recruited, especially by the French, to fight in Europe (e.g. the French recruited over 200,000 soldiers from their sparsely populated West African colonies). Many were killed but the African soldiers who returned home came back with new ideas and hopes and a changed attitude towards Europeans, effects felt even more strongly after the Second World War.

c) Economy. The start of the war caused serious economic problems in many areas which were suddenly prevented from trading with Germany (e.g. before the war seventy-five per cent of the vegetable oils from the British West African colonies were exported to Germany). Later the war had the effect of strengthening the trading links between the colonies and the European powers which ruled them, and of encouraging the development of communications and cash crops.

d) Rebellion. Excessive recruiting, economic problems and the fact that the war occurred just as many areas were beginning to feel the full impact of colonial rule produced widespread rebellions (e.g. in much of French West Africa). These rebellions showed the colonial powers the strength of opposition to colonial rule and contributed to changes in colonial policy immediately after the war.

e) The Mandate System. At the 1919–20 Versailles Peace Conference Germany's colonies were not returned to her, but were made the responsibility of the newly-created League of Nations under a system known as the Mandate System. The victorious powers (mostly Britain and France) were to govern Germany's ex-colonies on behalf of the League of Nations which was to ensure that real development and not exploitation took place. The new idea of imperial responsibility in the Mandate System was soon accepted, at least in theory, by the colonial powers, and was further elaborated in the influential books of Lugard, *The Dual Mandate in Tropical Africa*, and Sarraut, *La mise en valeur des colonies françaises*, published in the early 1920s.

Main types of colonial rule

More detailed examples of the working of the various types of colonial rule in different parts of Africa will be given in the later regional chapters. All that is intended here is to indicate some of the common features of colonial rule and the general policies of the major colonial powers.

After the First World War colonial policies became more uniform with most of the earlier extremes disappearing, and colonial powers learning and borrowing from one another. Central government varied little and changed little between the First and Second World Wars. Most colonies were headed by a Governor assisted by some form of legislative or advisory council. Each colony was divided into administrative units (given various names) headed by a European political officer and further divided into smaller sub-units. Central government was entirely in European hands until after the Second World War when the colonial powers, except Belgium and Portugal, began to prepare for eventual independence by making increasing use of European-style democratic institutions.

Almost everywhere there were too few European political officers to make direct rule possible (e.g. there were only about 200 British political officers in relatively densely populated Nigeria in 1925, and only just over 200 French political officers in the whole of French Equatorial Africa in the 1930s). This lack of political officers necessitated the use of Africans in local government in one way or another. Another very important factor in determining colonial policies was the presence or absence of white settlers: only in Algeria and South Africa did white settlers form as much as ten per cent of the population, but throughout Central Africa, where there were sizeable white settler communities, they exerted a strong influence on colonial governments.

By the 1920s it is possible to distinguish three main types of colonial policy (especially in the colonies of exploitation). These are usually called assimilation, indirect rule and paternalism. The comprehensive policy known as assimilation is often linked with the French and means that the Africans should be developed in every way as imitations of Europeans. In the vast colonial empires of the twentieth century, few people regarded full-scale personal or cultural assimilation possible, but administrative, political and economic assimilation remained the dominant aspect of colonial policy in many parts of Africa. Indirect rule is a much more precise term referring to a method of local government. Indirect rule is often seen as the opposite of assimilation since it means ruling through traditional rulers and institutions with change kept to a minimum. The vague term paternalism (often called 'association' in connection with the French) refers to the broad middle course between assimilation and indirect rule and means the reorganisation of society as much as is necessary for full exploitation.

a) British policies. It is difficult to generalise about British colonial rule since there was considerable regional variation. The old-established settler colonies of Natal and the Cape were special cases, as were Egypt and Sudan. For their remaining colonies in Africa, the British had by the 1920s developed a uniform theory, although great variety remained in practice. The British system was very decentralised, much being left to the initiative of individual Governors. The central government of each colony was basically similar headed by a Governor assisted by an executive council and a legislative council. This basic structure was modified and complicated in those countries of Central and East Africa with a significant white settler population (especially Kenya and Rhodesia – now Zimbabwe). The British were uncertain as to the role of white settler minorities and, despite the South African example, handed Rhodesia over to the white settlers in 1923 and almost made the same mistake in Kenya. The small coastal colonies held by Britain before the partition (e.g. Freetown, Lagos) were ruled as crown colonies with strong assimilationist elements (e.g. British law and citizenship). The rest of Africa under British rule, the huge areas conquered during the partition, were controlled largely by indirect rule methods.

Indirect rule had often been used before by the British (e.g. in India). It began to be used in Africa as the only possible method of administering huge, rapidly conquered, little-known areas cheaply. The British came to regard indirect rule as the only possible method of local government and tried to introduce it even where it was unsuitable. Indirect rule often produced stagnation and delayed progress and provided no role for the expanding western-educated elite. It worked effectively only where there were already strong, respected traditional rulers. In areas where indirect rule proved a complete disaster, the British tended towards a paternalist attitude.

b) French policies. The French conquered a huge empire in North-west, West and Central Africa during the partition. Their territories in West and Central Africa were ruled as two federations, French West Africa and French Equatorial Africa. The French tended towards assimilationist policies and, when they realised full-scale assimilation was neither possible nor desirable, a form of paternalism usually called association. Only a very small proportion of the population, mostly from the coastal areas of North Africa and the Four Communes of Senegal, were affected by full-scale personal assimilation. Administrative and economic assimilation were more widespread: the colonies were regarded as 'Overseas France', were highly centralised, were divided into local government units of approximately equal area, and were very closely linked with France economically. Many African states were destroyed during the French conquest (e.g. the Mandinka and Tokolor empires). Traditional rulers were not respected and traditional boundaries and methods of selecting chiefs were ignored. The French used indirect rule methods as little as possible, but had to in order to control some areas (e.g. parts of the Sahara desert).

c) Portuguese policies. The Portuguese were the first Europeans to establish colonies on the African coast and the last European power to grant independence and withdraw from Africa. Several factors (e.g. Portugal's poverty and her dictatorial government under Salazar 1933–68) made centralisation and repression the main aspects of her colonial policy. There was even less social and economic development than in the rest of Africa and a harsh system of forced labour known as the 'shibalo' system was widely used. The Portuguese colonies were closely linked to the mother country politically and economically, very little authority was left to traditional rulers, and virtually no opportunities for education were provided. The vast majority of the population remained 'indigenas' with no rights, and the small assimilated elite known as the 'assimilado' never numbered more than half a per cent of the population (e.g. there were 4,550 assimilado in Mozambique in 1956 out of a population of six million). Large-scale white settlement was encouraged during the Salazar period, and this created another problem for the peoples under Portuguese rule.

d) Belgian policies. King Leopold II of Belgium was forced to hand over his private empire in Central Africa to the Belgian Government in 1908 as a result of the scandal caused by the inhuman activities of his agents and concession-aire trading companies. The Colonial Charter of 1908 laid down the basic principles underlying Belgian colonial rule for the next fifty years. The huge Congo (now Zaïre) was Belgium's only colony, and so Belgium was able to concentrate on providing it with a centralised, paternalist, highly planned colonial system. The Congo was divided into provinces each ruled by a Governor with a Governor-General in overall charge. There was no alienation of land and few permanent European residents, but little attempt was made to encourage unity. Some aspects of indirect rule were used, but the Belgians used more European officers than other colonial powers (over 10,000 Belgian administrative officers by 1960) and were therefore able to rule more directly.

e) German policies. German colonial rule, which lasted only a quarter of a century, was in its early stages very repressive and paternalistic. White settle-ment was encouraged and land was set aside for white settlers especially where railways were to be built. The Herero rebellion in Namibia and the Maji Maji war in Tanzania led the Germans to rethink their colonial policies in 1907. From 1907 onwards considerable achievements were made in such areas as education, railway-building and agricultural research, but the outbreak of the First World War in 1914 prevented the full development of these policies.

14

Colonial rule: economic developments

As in the last chapter, we will again be dealing with general aspects relevant to large areas of Africa. Most of what follows is largely concerned with tropical Africa, the northern coastal areas and the southern tip of Africa being economically, as in other ways, rather special cases.

The colonial economy: main features

The economic development of Africa during the colonial period varied considerably depending on the resources available, world demand, the interests and policies of the colonial powers and the presence or absence of a white settler community. Nevertheless it is possible to distinguish certain general themes important throughout Africa:

a) Finance. All the colonial powers expected their colonies to be financially self-sufficient, a difficult task since both government and army were expensive. Large-scale investment and financial aid from the colonial powers were not available to pay for and speed up economic development until after the Second World War.

b) Exploitation. All the colonial powers exploited Africa. Economic factors had been major causes for Europe's partition of Africa in the late nineteenth century, so it should not be surprising that economic exploitation was a major aspect of colonial rule. African colonies were expected to supply cheap raw materials (cash crops and minerals) and to buy the surplus manufactured goods of European industries. This fundamental colonial economic policy, known by the French as the Colonial Pact, produced exploitation rather than development and has been a major factor in causing many of the economic difficulties facing present-day Africa. All development before the Second World War was aimed at benefiting the European colonial power rather than the peoples of Africa.

c) Planning. Colonial governments provided little long-term economic planning until after the Second World War. Most involved themselves in social and economic matters as little as possible (a policy known as 'laissez-faire'), leaving economic matters largely in the hands of businessmen.

d) Main stages. In many parts of Africa rapid economic change and growth began during the first decades of colonial rule (e.g. the building of railways and the expansion of cash crop production). These early developments were interrupted by the First World War and the readjustments necessary immediately after it. World prices for most of Africa's exports were high in the 1920s and rapid progress took place, but the world economic depression around 1930 caused great problems and delayed further development. Africa had not fully recovered from the depression when the Second World War began in 1939. This war stimulated certain aspects of Africa's economy and started off a period of rapid growth and expansion in the 1940s and 1950s.

e) Change. The colonial period was one of great economic change: there was a change-over from subsistence to cash crop farming, an expansion of trade, greater links with the world economy, and improvement in transport. Some of these changes had begun before the establishment of colonial rule (e.g. the production and export of cash crops along parts of the West African coast) and would almost certainly have continued and spread even without colonial rule. Moreover many parts of Africa which offered little economic gain to the Europeans were neglected and changed little, and only in a very few areas (e.g. in the cocoa-growing areas of southern Ghana and south-western Nigeria and in the cotton-growing areas of Uganda) did the standard of living improve significantly.

f) Determining factors. Factors other than geographic ones, e.g. the availability of resources, did much to determine the pace and type of economic development. Colonial governments found their task easier in those areas with an existing export economy (e.g. the West African coast), and most difficult in those areas (e.g. most of central Africa) where there was very little on which to build and where finance was a great problem in the early decades (e.g. the short-lived but ruthless attempt to base the economy on wild rubber in Zaïre and Angola). Another crucial factor was land and whether it was alienated to white settlers: where influential settler communities developed (e.g. Kenya, Angola), the economy was generally even more exploitative and of even less benefit to Africans than in areas without a large settler community (e.g. Uganda, West Africa).

Improved communications

In order to be financially self-sufficient, colonies had to produce sufficient exports, and to make this possible a transport revolution was needed. One of the most important things which caused change during the colonial period, and upon which all other economic development was dependent, was the transformation in communications in the early twentieth century. Previously transport had been by water where there were navigable rivers, or on foot (human or animal). If the interior were to be opened up to world trade, a much speedier and cheaper form of transport to the coast was needed. This was provided by the railways.

During the half-century 1880–1930, over 40,000 kilometres of railway were built in Africa. Most of the important main-lines were completed (or nearly so) by the outbreak of the First World War (e.g. Wadi Halfa to Khartoum 1899; Addis Ababa to Djibouti 1917; Lagos to Kano 1910; Matadi to Kinshasa 1898; Mombasa to Kisumu 1901; and Dar es Salaam to Kigoma 1914). The First World War interrupted railway building, but important extensions to the rail network were added in the 1920s and 1930s (e.g. the Benguela railway was extended to Shaba, the 'Uganda' railway reached Kampala, the eastern line was built in Nigeria, and several railways were built in Sudan). Only South Africa and coastal North Africa developed a dense rail network: Nigeria, Sudan and Zaïre had several lines, whilst most colonies could afford only a single main line, or in some cases no railway at all.

Some railways were initially built for political reasons (e.g. access from the coast in order to establish control) as much as for economic reasons, but all soon produced important economic effects. At the coastal termini of the railways (e.g. Dakar, Lagos, Lobito, Mombasa), deep-water harbours were constructed to facilitate external trade.

The railways built during the colonial period share certain common features.

a) There was little European investment in African railways: the railways were paid for almost entirely by African taxes.
b) Most railways ran from the interior to the coast to suit the needs of the export economy.
c) African interests and needs were not taken into consideration: railways were built only to those areas economically important to the Europeans because they supplied cash crops or minerals.
d) There were few rail-links between territories.

Wherever railways were built their effects were revolutionary, but it must be remembered that huge areas remained far from any railway. The bicycle from the beginning of the colonial period and the motor car and lorry from the 1920s had a more widespread impact than the railways. Colonial governments were reluctant to build roads that would compete with government-owned railways, but roads were built in many areas where there were no railways, and feeder roads were provided to link areas to the railways.

These improvements in communications had important results.

a) They made possible a great increase in cash crop production (e.g. cotton in Uganda and ground-nuts in northern Nigeria and Senegal).
b) They facilitated the import and spread of European manufactured goods, which often meant severe competition for the African local manufacturer.
c) Mobility of population increased, and large-scale migration became possible.
d) With this mobility of population went rapid urbanisation, especially along the railways (e.g. Nairobi, Kinshasa, Lagos, Abidjan).
e) In some cases improved communications helped to create greater unity, by providing links between the different parts of the country (e.g. Nigeria).
f) The railways provided employment for many.
g) Improved communications facilitated the introduction of new ideas.

Raw materials

Once the railways had been built, colonial governments did everything possible to encourage the production of cash crops (e.g. ground-nuts, cotton, cocoa, coffee and sisal). In large areas of Africa the nineteenth-century subsistence economy was changed into a cash crop economy. Two very different types of agricultural development took place. Where there were few or no white settlers (e.g. West Africa) cash crop production was left in the hands of small-scale African farmers and progress was in some cases rapid (e.g. Ghana was the world's largest cocoa producer from 1911). In much of Central and East Africa, however, where white settlers were allowed to occupy much of the best land (e.g. the 40,000 square kilometre 'white highlands' of Kenya), the production of cash crops was concentrated in large, European-owned farms and little progress took place in African agriculture until the 1950s. The growth of a plantation-settler economy produced great problems for the areas affected when they moved towards independence – problems which still continue in Zimbabwe.

In addition to these two main types of agricultural development, other methods were used. The Gezira irrigation scheme in Sudan provides a good example of African cash crop production under strict European organisation and control. In much of Zaïre and French Equatorial Africa, land was handed over to large European concessionaire companies which used the most ruthless forms of exploitation, especially during the first decades of colonial rule.

Certain common features of agricultural development can be distinguished:

a) Government assistance to agriculture (e.g. research) was slight and concentrated entirely on cash crops to the exclusion of basic food crops.

b) Little attempt was made to diversify the economy, many colonies relying on only one major cash crop export (e.g. sisal in Tanzania and cocoa in Ghana), and so suffering greatly when world prices for their particular crop fell.

c) Large areas not considered suitable for cash crop production were neglected.

d) Where there were white settlers they had great advantages over African farmers (e.g. capital and the best land) and could produce higher yields.

e) Colonial government policy (especially concerning land and labour) was crucial in determining the pattern of agricultural development.

A lot of development also took place in mining, which was entirely controlled by a few large European companies (e.g. the United Africa Company owned all the mineral rights in northern Nigeria and the British South Africa Company controlled the mineral rights in the copper belt of Zambia). These companies paid very little tax to the colonial governments, most of their profits going to shareholders in Europe so that Africans benefited little from the introduction and expansion of mining. In some areas mining became a major source of employment (e.g. there were about 22,000 Africans employed in the copper mines of Zambia by 1930). Only in South Africa was the growth of mining accompanied by full-scale industrialisation and only there did mining completely dominate the economy.

Other important economic factors

a) Currency. During the first decades of colonial rule currency in the form first of coins and later notes, was gradually introduced, and a cash exchange economy largely replaced barter.

b) Trade. There was a great increase in import and export trade (e.g. the value of Kenya's exports increased from £0·3 million to £24·1 million between 1911 and 1951, and during the same period imports rose from £1.1 million to £50·6 million). Very little of this external trade was controlled by Africans. Huge monopolistic European companies (e.g. the French company SCOA and the Belgian company 'Union Minière') dominated every aspect of foreign trade. On a smaller scale, Africans were further deprived of trading opportunities by the spread of Lebanese traders in much of West Africa and Indians in much of Central and East Africa.

c) Industries. Only in South Africa was there any large-scale industrial development. Colonial governments did not encourage industrialisation since it would mean competition for European industries. In most of tropical Africa the only early industries were those necessary to process cash crops and minerals before export (e.g. cotton ginning). Only after the Second World War were factories producing such things as bricks, soap, beer and bread established, and right up to the time of independence most countries had few manufacturing industries. Several hydro-electricity projects were started in the 1950s (e.g. Kariba and Akosombo), and between 1948 and 1956 consumption of electricity in Africa trebled from 2,000 million kWh to 6,000 million kWh.

d) Land. At one extreme was South Africa where as much as eighty-eight per cent of the land was allocated to non-Africans and at the other extreme was West Africa where there was virtually no alienation of land. In most of Central and East Africa (e.g. Angola, Zimbabwe and Kenya) some of the best land was handed over to white settlers or European companies creating great social and political problems.

e) Labour. In most of Africa, various types of forced labour were used (e.g. the contract labourers sent by the Portuguese from Angola to Sao Tomé). Even when wages were paid they were often too low to attract workers without some degree of force (e.g. in the Enugu coal-mines in Nigeria). Although trade-unionism was strongly discouraged, several strikes occurred (e.g. strikes by railway workers in Senegal in 1925 and 1938), and in the 1940s trade-unionism expanded rapidly.

f) Development. There was a great shortage of capital to finance economic development except along the north coast, in South Africa and where there were valuable minerals. The colonial powers did little to finance development until the 1940s when both Britain (the Colonial Development and Welfare Act 1940) and France (FIDES 1946) began to provide some financial assistance.

g) Tax. All the European powers imposed taxation as soon as possible in order to raise revenue. Many Africans had to migrate (either temporarily or permanently) to find work in order to pay tax, and rapid urbanisation took place.

15

Social developments during the colonial period

Few historians have so far studied the causes and results of social, cultural and intellectual developments during the first half of the twentieth century. Undoubtedly colonial rule had important, often destructive, influences on many aspects of social life, but many colonial historians have exaggerated this social impact. The richness of traditional African culture has often been ignored in order to emphasise the so-called 'civilising' effects of colonial rule. Great changes occurred, especially in religion and education, but many basic features of African society survived the colonial period little altered.

Religious developments

In the late nineteenth and early twentieth centuries traditional ethnic religions were greatly weakened by the political, economic and social effects of colonial rule. In many areas this produced a religious vacuum rapidly filled by Islam or Christianity.

The spread of Islam

Islam had for many centuries been the dominant religion of much of northern Africa. During the colonial period it was consolidated in those areas where it was already established, and it also spread to neighbouring regions (e.g. it has been estimated that during the first half of the twentieth century the Muslim population of West Africa more than doubled). Many of the established brotherhoods (e.g. the Tijaniyya) greatly increased their strength and important new brotherhoods were founded (e.g. the Muridiyya in Senegal). During the partition and throughout the colonial period, Muslims often took the lead in opposing European domination (e.g. Senussiya resistance to the Italian occupation of Libya, and Somali resistance led by Muhammed Abdullah Hassan, 1864–1920, to British, Italian and Ethiopian expansion). In the strongly Muslim states of North Africa the relationship between Islam and modernisation was a major issue throughout the colonial period. Several aspects of the new colonial situation favoured the spread of Islam; e.g. military service and migration to towns meant separation from traditional religion and brought contact with Islam.

A few examples must be mentioned of the many various movements within Islam which developed partly in reaction to the colonial situation. The Muridiyya movement founded by Ahmadu Bamba in Senegal was an offshoot of the Qadiriyya brotherhood and soon gained large-scale support especially among the

Wolof. Ahmadu Bamba stressed the importance of work, and the rapid development of ground-nut production in Senegal was largely achieved by members of the Muridiyya. Initially the French opposed the Muridiyya movement, but the growing importance of its members in the Senegalese economy made the French try to cooperate with the Muridiyya leaders.

A more radical, militant form of Islam, known as Hamallism, developed in the French Sudan (now Mali) in the 1920s and 1930s. Hamallism was founded by Sheikh Hamallah at Nioro and was an attempt to return to original Tijaniyya Islam. The French strongly discouraged the movement and deported Sheikh Hamallah who died in exile in France in 1943. Hamallists played a major part in the development of radical nationalism after the Second World War.

The Ahmadiyya movement, regarded by the majority of Muslims as unorthodox, was founded in India in 1908. The Ahmadiyya movement organised itself along the same lines as a Christian missionary body, emphasised the value of European-style education, and gained its largest support among the Fante of Ghana.

The spread of Christianity

Christianity also spread rapidly during the colonial period. Christian missionaries had very limited success in the nineteenth century, but were greatly aided by the establishment of colonial rule. During the early decades of colonial rule the number of Christian missionaries in Africa increased greatly, and in all areas where Islam was not already firmly established, Christianity spread so rapidly that by 1960 there were over fifty million African Christians. The early missionaries opposed almost every aspect of traditional culture (e.g. polygamy and female circumcision), but so favourable was the colonial situation to the spread of world religions that large groups (e.g. most of the Igbo) rapidly adopted Christianity.

In the new, more racialist atmosphere of colonial domination, the nineteenth-century equality between European missionaries and Africans and the encouragement of African leadership in the church (e.g. the work of Bishop Samuel Ajayi Crowther in the Niger Delta) were abandoned. European missionaries were closely linked with European colonial rulers and church leadership was monopolised by Europeans until the 1950s (e.g. in Zaïre there were only five African priests by 1925). These factors, and the need to adapt Christianity to African society, led to the formation of many independent African churches free of European mission control.

Independent churches

During the colonial period as many as 5,000 independent church movements were founded, some gaining a very large following and today forming one of the most active areas of Christianity in Africa. Some of these churches grew out of the work and teachings of a founder-prophet (e.g. William Wade Harris in Liberia and the Ivory Coast, Simon Kimbangu in Zaïre, and Alice Lenshina in Central Africa), while others were distinctive in their emphasis on the power of prayer (e.g. the Aladura churches in south-western Nigeria and the Zionist churches in South Africa). These churches were in many ways an expression of nationalist opposition to European rule and were often distrusted and persecuted by the colonial authorities. The brutal crushing of the rebellion led by the Yao preacher John Chilembwe in Malawi in 1915 showed the dangers of open religious opposition to colonial rule and led many churches to emphasise hopes of the next world rather than the inequalities and injustices of this world.

The following are three examples of the many important African churches created during the colonial period:

a) Aladura. Many churches developed in Yorubaland and neighbouring areas (e.g. the Christ Apostolic Church, the Cherubim and Seraphim Church) collectively known as the Aladura churches because of their emphasis on the need for and value of prayer. These churches began with the preaching of J. B. Sadane at Ijebu Ode in 1918 and were greatly strengthened and expanded by a revival movement led by Joseph Babalola in the 1930s.

b) WatchTower. Very important in much of Central Africa was the WatchTower movement, an offshoot of the American-based Jehovah's Witnesses. Watch-Tower was founded by Elliot Kamwana in Malawi in about 1908 and, although often persecuted, soon spread to neighbouring areas. It became very influential in eastern Zaïre where it was known as Kitawala.

c) Kimbanguism. In western Zaïre, especially among the Kongo people, the Kimbanguist church (today one of the largest in Africa) was founded in 1921 by the prophet Simon Kimbangu. He was imprisoned by the Belgian authorities and remained in prison until his death in 1951, but his church spread rapidly.

Education

Probably the most important cause of social and cultural change and one of the major impacts of Christian missionary work was the spread of European-style education. Lack of finance limited educational growth, and educational systems unsuitable to African needs were often produced. During the first two decades of the twentieth century education was left almost entirely to the Christian missionaries who concentrated on primary education and basic literacy. Mission education soon produced an educated elite highly critical of colonial rule.

Very little government education was provided until after the First World War and even then only very small amounts were spent on education. A few special schools for training administrators were established (e.g. Katsina College in northern Nigeria, the Ponty school in Dakar, and Gordon College in Sudan), and the men who completed courses there often played a major part in the growth of nationalism. The presence of white settlers delayed the growth of secondary education (e.g. Kenya had no government secondary schools in 1938 while Nigeria had forty-two). Secondary education was available to more students in British-controlled Africa than in the parts of Africa under French, Belgian or Portuguese colonial rule (e.g. in the whole of French West Africa there were only two secondary schools in the 1930s and in the Belgian Congo – now Zaïre – virtually no secondary education was provided throughout the colonial period). In many countries educational opportunities were unevenly distributed (e.g. in Nigeria, missionary education was not allowed in the Muslim areas of the north and few government schools were provided as an alternative).

Much more rapid educational development took place after the Second World War, as education played a major part in the development plans started in the late 1940s. Many primary teacher training centres were opened in the 1940s and secondary education expanded rapidly in the 1950s. Except for Fourah Bay College in Sierra Leone, there were no universities in Africa outside Egypt and South Africa until after the Second World War. In the late 1940s the British opened university colleges at Ibadan, Khartoum, Makerere and Achimota, but in the rest of colonial Africa facilities for post-secondary education remained virtually non-existent until after independence.

The following table shows how varied was the amount of education available, and how limited was education even towards the end of the colonial period.

Percentage of children of school age attending school 1955		
	Primary	Secondary
Ghana	48%	20%
Kenya	29%	2%
Chad	3%	0·2%

Colonial education was limited not only in quantity but also in type: virtually no scientific or technical education was provided and syllabuses remained very European-biased. In addition, most education was conducted in the language of the colonial power; this provided a common language in countries with a great variety of African languages, but it also led to various problems after independence.

Migration and urbanisation

Improved communications enabled much greater movement of people. Widespread migration took place usually towards the railways, the mining areas and the cities, for a variety of reasons: people went to seek work to pay the taxes, to avoid some of the worst features of colonial rule (e.g. forced labour), and to escape the limitations of traditional society. Much of this migration was at first temporary, but soon became permanent, except in the very special South African conditions. In much of West Africa there was a movement from the savannah areas southwards to the coast (e.g. the migration of Mossi from Upper Volta to Ivory Coast and Ghana), and in Central Africa many moved to the mining areas of Zaïre and Zambia.

One major aspect of the movement of peoples was the rapid growth of towns, especially after the Second World War. Old-established towns (e.g. Mombasa, Algiers, Ibadan) expanded greatly and new towns (e.g. Casablanca, Nairobi, Kinshasa) soon grew into large cities. In these growing towns, peoples of different ethnic groups were mixed together, family and ethnic ties were weakened, and European ideas and influences were more widespread. In the towns there were more opportunities for education and jobs, and a large wage-earning class developed; but there was also a lot of suffering from overcrowding and poor housing. All of these things contributed to, and made the towns the centres of, nationalist movements.

Other aspects

The following were among other social developments during the colonial period.

a) Population. During the partition and the early decades of colonial rule serious epidemics affected much of Africa. Animal diseases (e.g. rinderpest) destroyed cattle in much of Central Africa, devastating cattle-keeping societies, and human diseases (e.g. smallpox and sleeping sickness) killed hundreds of thousands. These epidemics, the last years of slave trading and the wars against the Europeans reduced the population in many parts of Africa. Populations began to expand in the 1920s and this expansion grew more rapid from the 1940s onwards.

b) Health. One cause for the increase in population after about 1920 was an improvement in health facilities reducing the death rate. Much work in the field of health was left to the missionaries, for colonial governments spent very little on health (e.g. in 1936 there were only 3,500 hospital beds for Africans in Nigeria and under 1,000 in Ghana).

c) Slavery. The establishment of colonial rule put an end to the various slave trades in Africa, and more gradually slavery itself was abolished. All colonial governments claimed to oppose slavery; but since they needed soldiers and cheap labour, they often encouraged various types of forced labour very similar to slavery.

d) Basic rights. In most of colonial Africa, people were denied their basic freedoms of speech, movement, and political association until after the Second World War and in some areas (e.g. Portuguese-controlled Africa) until independence. All colonial governments were forms of alien domination imposed by force and all were in varying degrees repressive. The 'indigénat', used by the French, by which people could be imprisoned without trial, is just one example of the unjust and inhuman way in which Africans were often treated during the colonial period and are still treated today in South Africa.

16

Northern Africa c. 1900–60

In this chapter we shall consider the main twentieth-century developments in both North-west Africa (Morocco, Algeria, Tunisia and Libya) and North-east Africa (Egypt, Sudan, Ethiopia and Somalia). Islam is common to the whole area (except Ethiopia) and played a major role in the opposition to European domination. The most important aspects of this topic are the rise of nationalism, which developed earlier in Muslim northern Africa than in tropical Africa, and the long-drawn-out struggle for independence. The independence movement did not follow the same pattern throughout this huge region (e.g. Egypt gained self-government in 1922, Algeria was not independent until 1962 and Ethiopia was under colonial rule for less than a decade), and so it will be necessary to outline the main events in each country.

North-west Africa

The establishment of a French protectorate over most of Morocco in 1912 brought the last independent part of the Maghrib under European control. France ruled the whole area except Libya (controlled by Italy) and a small part of northern Morocco (controlled by Spain).

The whole area was influenced by similar factors during the colonial period.

a) There was fierce resistance to European domination, for example the Kabylia rebellion in Algeria in 1871, the Senussiya war against the Italians until the early 1930s, and the Berber rebellion led by Abd al Qrim in the Rif Mountains of northern Morocco in the early 1920s.

b) The importance of the region to the European governments was strategic (they wanted to control the southern coast of the Mediterranean Sea) rather than economic (for oil was not discovered until the 1950s).

c) The majority of the population were Arabic-speaking Muslims. Islam played an important part in the nationalist movements of the various countries, and the area was linked to and influenced by the rest of the Arab Muslim world (e.g. by pan-Islamic ideas originating from the Al-Azhar University in Cairo).

d) Because it was close to Europe and in parts was suitable for European-style agriculture, there were many European settlers in all four countries. By the end of the 1930s there were over a million white settlers in Algeria, about 200,000 in Morocco, nearly 200,000 in Tunisia and about 50,000 in sparsely-populated Libya. Much of the best land was taken by the settlers and this forced many people to move into the cities. Colonial administration was strongly influenced by the settlers, and resentment against the racialist arrogance of the settlers strengthened nationalism.

e) There was considerable economic development during the colonial period (e.g. roads, railways and ports were built), but most of it benefited the European settlers rather than the Africans.

f) Nationalism developed as a reaction to the political, economic and social conditions of colonial rule and was influenced by both Islam and by European-style education. Improved communications, hostility towards the settlers, the growth of an urban working class, and the greater unity produced by the whole of each country being brought under one authority all contributed to the growth of nationalism.

Morocco

Morocco was ruled by the French as a protectorate: the sultan and traditional forms of government continued, but the French increasingly ignored the protectorate treaty and exercised more and more direct control. It took the French many years to bring the whole country under French rule and the Spanish did not fully control their small northern protectorate until after the Rif rebellion of the early 1920s. Marshal Lyautey, the French Resident-General of Morocco from 1912 to 1925 was very able: he introduced indirect rule methods, ruling through the sultan and his 'caids' (chiefs), and he respected Islam and Moroccan culture. During this period law and order was established throughout the country, economic progress was made and European settlers were discouraged. Unfortunately, from the late 1920s onwards, the French tried to rule more directly and undermined much of the work done by Lyautey.

The first nationalist groups in Morocco were founded in the 1920s by such leaders as Mohammed el Fassi. Lack of unity and French repression prevented much progress. Nationalist feeling was strengthened by several unpopular French measures, for example the encouragement given to Christian missionaries and the Berber 'Dahir' of 1930 which tried to divide Berber and Arab by secularising justice. In 1927 Mohammed V became sultan and for a few years cooperated reluctantly with the French; he was waiting until the time was ready for him to assume the leadership of the nationalist movement.

In 1943 the Istiqlal or Independence Party was formed with the sultan's support. During the Second World War Morocco fought for the Free French and many thousand Moroccans were killed freeing France from German control. Sultan Mohammed and the nationalists expected French concessions in return after the war, but in the late 1940s the French Government, urged on by the settlers, attempted to tighten their control and destroy the nationalist movement. The French tried to weaken the sultan's authority and encouraged the ambitions of their supporter, the overmighty Caid of Marrakesh, Thami al-Glawi. Mohammed V's popularity among his subjects increased and the French became so alarmed by the growth of nationalism, centred on the sultan, that in 1953 they deposed and exiled him. This produced widespread protest and an army of liberation was formed. The French, fighting a losing war in Indo-China and beginning to come under attack in Algeria, could not afford to fight to retain Morocco. In 1955 Sultan Mohammed V was restored, and in 1956 Morocco became independent.

Algeria

Algeria had been gradually conquered by France during the nineteenth century and was ruled, not as a protectorate, but as a part of France. The economy and most of the fertile land was controlled by about a million European settlers (known as 'colons') who maintained close links with, and great influence in, France. These settlers (the largest white settler community in Africa except South Africa) resisted the growth of nationalism as long and as strongly as possible. It was largely because of these settlers that Algeria, the first part of North Africa to be conquered by Europeans, was the last to gain independence and then only after the bloodiest war in colonial Africa.

Throughout the first half of the twentieth century the French settlers in Algeria used their influence in France to block reforms favourable to Algerians (e.g. in both 1919 and 1938 the granting of greater rights to the Muslim population was prevented). Several nationalist parties (e.g. the 'Etoile Nord-Africaine' and the 'Parti Populaire Algérien') were created in the 1920s and 1930s, Hadj Messali being the most important of the early nationalist leaders. There were also in these decades pro-French political groups (e.g. that led by Ferhat Abbas) who favoured assimilation and wanted equal rights within France. So oppressive was French rule and so opposed to any sort of equality were the settlers that by the 1940s even these groups were criticising the French and demanding independence.

In 1945 violence broke out between Muslim Algerians and white settlers. The French reacted with brutal repression and the nationalist groups continued their activities in secret. The French were prepared to make concessions in Morocco and Tunisia, but were determined to fight to keep Algeria. There was no hope of making progress towards independence peacefully and in 1954 full-scale war broke out. For the next seven years the well-organised FLN ('Front de Libéra-tion Nationale') supported by the bulk of the population fought against half a million French troops. During this long and bloody struggle the Algerian people developed a strong sense of nationhood. In 1958 the Fifth Republic was created in France with General de Gaulle as President. De Gaulle wanted to finish the Algerian war and began to make moves towards independence, despite the strong opposition of the settlers who formed themselves into a secret army to prevent peace. A cease-fire was finally agreed in 1962, and Algeria became independent and was led by Ben Bella.

Tunisia

Tunisia, smaller and more homogenous than the other Maghrib countries, was ruled by France as a protectorate from 1881. The government of the Bey continued in theory, but, as in Morocco, the French increasingly tried to rule directly. Nationalism began early in Tunisia: the first African-owned newspaper, 'Al Hadira', started in 1888 and the Young Tunisia Party was formed in 1908. This party, the most influential leader of which was Shaik al Thaalbi, was known as the 'Destour' (Constitution) party from 1920. The French repressed this early nationalism, deporting most of the Destour leaders in the 1920s, and the growth of nationalism was further delayed by disagreements between the western-educated elite and the Muslim leaders, the 'ulema'.

In 1934 a lawyer, Habib Bourgiba, founded the more radical Neo-Destour party and from then on dominated the movement towards independence. He was a brilliant leader and a realist, and gradually put increasing pressure on the French to grant concessions. But under pressure from nearly a quarter of a million French settlers, the French repressed the nationalists and finally arrested Bourgiba in 1952. This led to widescale rioting which the French found difficult to control. Facing serious problems in Indo-China and Algeria in the mid-1950s, the French were in no position to fight to retain Tunisia. Tunisia was granted independence in 1956 under the leadership of Bourgiba and the Neo-Destour party. The Bey played no part in the nationalist struggle, and in 1957 the monarchy was abolished and a republic was established.

Libya

The Italians had to fight for over twenty years to conquer the three regions of Tripolitania, Cyrenaica and Fezzan, which make up Libya, and firm Italian control lasted only a decade, the 1930s. There was no attempt to develop a European-educated elite and only the white settlers benefited from Italian rule. Italy was defeated in the Second World War, during which the Senussiya leader, Sayyid Idris, supported Italy's enemies (Britain, France and America). After the war Libya became the responsibility of the United Nations, and, after several years of discussion during which Britain, France and Italy competed for control, the United Nations granted independence in 1951. A constitutional assembly declared Sayyid Idris king.

Egypt and Sudan

Egypt

British rule in Egypt was different from British rule elsewhere because the British occupation in 1882 was meant to be temporary. Egypt remained nominally a part of the Ottoman Empire until 1914 and already possessed a well established and largely nationalist-educated elite. The government of the khedive and his ministers continued in theory, but in practice real power was in the hands of the British Consul-General, and Egypt was in all but name a part of the British Empire. British rule through the khedival government was a distinct type of indirect rule and there was very little British interference in many aspects of government (e.g. the judiciary and local government).

Lord Cromer was British Consul-General from 1883 to 1907. He tried to simplify all aspects of the complex and wasteful khedival government, but was most concerned with finance. Egypt was made solvent and some economic progress was made (e.g. the Aswan Dam was completed in 1902), but industry was neglected, very little was spent on education and health, and few Egyptians were appointed to the senior civil service.

During his period of office, nationalist opposition to the British occupation gained strength. The pan-Islamic ideas of Jamal al-Din Afghani, resentment at British control of Suez Canal revenue, and the 1906 Dinshawai incident when several Egyptians were unjustly hanged all helped the growth of nationalism.

Kitchener's attempts to crush nationalism failed and the outbreak of the First World War, which led to the creation of a full British protectorate, further increased opposition to the British.

Saad Zaghlul, the main nationalist leader, formed a party known as the 'Wafd' in 1918. In 1920 the British deported Zaghlul, serious rioting broke out and a British commission of enquiry recommended giving in to nationalist demands. In 1922 Egypt gained a limited form of independence with the khedive becoming king. The opposition of the Wafd party led the king (first Fuad and then Faruk) into close cooperation with the British. In 1936 Egypt became fully independent, but Britain retained control of the Suez Canal Zone and continued to interfere in Egyptian affairs. So unpopular were both the king and the Wafd party that many supported radical movements such as the Muslim Brotherhood.

Egypt's defeat by Israel in 1948 further discredited the king and the Wafd government, and in 1952 the army, led by Neguib, seized control and established a republic. In 1956 the British were driven out of the Suez Canal Zone, and under the leadership of Nasser rapid progress was made in land reform, industrial development, education and health.

Sudan

In 1898 the British, using a largely Egyptian army, defeated the Mahdist state and established joint British and Egyptian control (called the Anglo-Egyptian Condominium) over Sudan. It was many years before all parts of huge Sudan were brought under control (e.g. Darfur was not conquered until 1916). Real power was kept by the British: all Governor-Generals and most senior civil servants were British, causing considerable Egyptian resentment. During the Condominium period, indirect rule methods were used and the non-Muslim southern districts were administered separately from the Muslim north and centre. There was some economic progress (e.g. railways were built and the Gezira irrigation scheme was started), but little education was provided (e.g. Gordon College in Khartoum was the only secondary school until 1946).

The growth of Sudanese nationalism was encouraged and much influenced by rivalries between the joint foreign rulers, Britain and Egypt. Ethnic and religious divisions, especially between the Ansar (supporters of the Mahdi) and Khatmiyya brotherhoods, delayed the growth of nationalism. The first modern political parties were formed in 1943: the Ashiqqa party led by Ismail el Azhari was supported by the Khatmiyya and wanted union with Egypt; the Umma party led by Sayyid Abd al-Rahman al-Mahdi was supported by the Ansar and wanted full independence.

After the Second World War Sudan moved rapidly towards independence and support for the idea of union with Egypt weakened. A legislative assembly was set up in 1948, el Azhari became the first prime minister in 1954 with an all-Sudanese cabinet, and in 1956 Sudan became an independent republic. It was soon faced by civil war between the north and the south.

Ethiopia and Somalia

Ethiopia

The death of the Emperor Menelik II in 1913 began a period of confusion and conflict. His successor, Lij Iyasu, was incapable and unpopular, and he was overthrown by the rases in 1916. Menelik's daughter, Zauditu, became empress with Ras Tafari as regent. Ras Tafari, son of Ras Makonnen and great-grandson of Sahle Selassie of Shoa, dominated Ethiopian history for more than half a century. His modernising ideas were opposed by the empress, the Church and the rases, but, despite this opposition, he succeeded in becoming emperor in 1930 as Haile Selassie.

By this time Italy, ruled by the dictator Mussolini, was looking for an opportunity to revenge her defeat at Adowa. Haile Selassie tried to avoid the Italian threat through diplomacy, but in 1934 the Italians used the Wal Wal incident (a minor disagreement over the control of a well near the Ethiopia-Somalia border) as a pretext for war. Haile Selassie was given no support by the League of Nations and in 1935 the Italians invaded and conquered Ethiopia driving Haile Selassie into exile. Italian rule was hated and, as a result of the Second World War, the Italians were driven out in 1941 and Haile Selassie was restored.

During his long reign as emperor (1930–74) Haile Selassie continued many of the reforms begun by Menelik II and made the monarchy the centre of reforms in all fields.

a) He issued a constitution in 1931 and a new one in 1955, but representative institutions were given little power and real control remained firmly in the emperor's hands.

b) Communications were improved and trade was increased.

c) Slavery was gradually abolished.

d) Education was expanded (by 1957 there were twenty-four secondary schools).

Haile Selassie was an inspiration to nationalists throughout Africa and played a leading role in African affairs. But his autocratic rule caused opposition, and in 1974 he was overthrown by a military coup and the monarchy was abolished.

Somalia

The British in the north and the Italians in the east gradually gained control of Somalia in the early decades of the twentieth century. Fierce resistance to European conquest was led by Muhammed Abdullah Hassan, the founder of modern Somali nationalism. British and Italian control remained loose and in 1941 the British occupied Italian Somaliland. After the Second World War, the United Nations, after much debate, handed the Italian part back to Italy in 1950 as a trust territory for ten years. During the 1950s great progress was made, and in 1960 both British and Italian Somaliland gained independence and united into a single Somali state.

17

West Africa c. 1900–60

By the early twentieth century the whole of West Africa, except Liberia, was divided up among the European powers. The French conquered more than three-quarters of West Africa (over 4,500,000 square kilometres), but much of this huge area was sparsely populated and economically unproductive desert and semi-desert. Britain's four West African colonies (Nigeria, Ghana, Sierra Leone and The Gambia) covered about 1,250,000 square kilometres, but were much more densely populated and economically more valuable. The only parts of West Africa not under French or British rule were the small countries of Togo (ruled by the Germans until the First World War and then divided between the British and the French), Guinea-Bissau ruled by the Portuguese, and independent Liberia.

French rule

From their old-established base in Senegal, the French, during the partition, conquered a huge area, the present-day countries of Senegal, Mauritania, Mali, Niger, Upper Volta, Benin, Ivory Coast and Guinea. The following are among the most important features of French rule in West Africa.

a) Basic policy. Every aspect of French rule was influenced by the basic policy of assimilation (see Chapter 13). Full-scale personal assimilation was used only in the four communes of Senegal (St. Louis, Rufisque, Gorée and Dakar). Elsewhere immediate full assimilation was neither practical nor financially possible and so from 1900 to 1946 a policy known as association was used, reorganising African society to suit the needs of exploitation and using administrative and economic assimilation.

   Personal assimilation failed, as it was bound to, since habits, culture, tradition and way of life cannot quickly be replaced by others developed in a different environment. Economic and administrative assimilation (which were easier to enforce) weakened or destroyed many valuable aspects of traditional society and culture, and created very close links with France, which complicated the movement towards independence and has created problems since independence.

b) Central government. In stages between 1895 and 1904 all the French territories were united into a highly centralised federation, the AOF ('Afrique Occidentale Française'). The federation was created in order to prevent conflicts, provide a united military command, simplify French control and for economic reasons (so that the more productive areas such as Senegal could help finance the poorer inland areas). The Governor-General, with his capital at Dakar, possessed great powers: he alone could communicate directly with the French Government in Paris and he controlled almost all civil service appointments, such federal matters as the army, customs and justice, and a large federal budget. Nevertheless, the Governor-General was closely controlled by the French Government and possessed little freedom of action.

c) Local government. The French ignored traditional boundaries and divided the whole of French West Africa into 'cercles', each with approximately the same size and population, each administered by a 'commandant de cercle', and each divided into subdivisions under a 'chef de subdivision'. The French used more political officers than the British and almost everywhere the traditional rulers were either destroyed or reduced to a very subordinate position; they were used merely to carry out such unpleasant tasks as tax-collecting and raising forced labour. In some areas the French tried to rule indirectly in cooperation with the leaders of Muslim groups such as the Tijaniyya and the Muridiyya.

d) The four communes. The four communes of Senegal were ruled quite differently from the rest of French West Africa. There the French systems of education and local government were firmly established and the inhabitants were French citizens with full rights, including that of electing a representative to the Chamber of Deputies in Paris.

e) Basic rights. Elsewhere the inhabitants were subjects, who were denied basic freedoms (e.g. of movement and of speech), were liable to forced labour and imprisonment without trial (the 'indigénat'), and were very heavily taxed. Only a very few got the chance of education, but the small educated elite that was created was better treated than the elite in British areas.

British rule

In 1914 northern and southern Nigeria were amalgamated (for financial reasons and to create a unified railway system) leaving the British with four territories in West Africa. Each was cut off from the others by French territory and they were ruled as completely separate units. Each was composed of a small coastal colony ruled directly and a much larger protectorate ruled indirectly. The governor of each territory had considerable freedom of action and was assisted by a legislative council and an executive council, which in the early colonial period were made up entirely of British officials. The British administration remained aloof from the people they were governing and, until the Second World War, did little to prepare the way for eventual independence. The growing educated elite in the coastal areas was treated with suspicion and even contempt and was excluded from participation in the administration.

At first there was a great variety of methods of local government, but by the 1920s the success (as far as the British were concerned) of Lugard's system of indirect rule (see Chapter 13) in northern Nigeria led British administrators (e.g. Guggisberg in Ghana and Palmer in The Gambia) to try and introduce indirect rule even where it was obviously unsuitable. The British tried to preserve what their very presence was changing and where indirect rule worked most smoothly (e.g. northern Nigeria) there was stagnation. To illustrate its working, indirect rule in two contrasting areas will be considered.

Indirect rule in the Muslim emirates of northern Nigeria

When Lugard conquered the Sokoto Caliphate in the first years of the twentieth century, lack of men and money necessitated the use of indirect rule. Moreover the Sokoto Caliphate already possessed a highly developed and efficient system of administration headed by the emirs, and was therefore suited to indirect rule. Once the British had assured the emirs that they did not intend to interfere with Islam, it was reasonably easy for the British to take over Sokoto's role of supervising the strong, respected emirs. A Resident or District Officer (DO) was sent to each emirate headquarters to advise and supervise the emir's administration. Lugard expected the DO's to adapt and modernise existing institutions, but many DOs saw their role as that of preservers rather than modifiers, falsely assuming that African society was fixed and unchanging. The emirs appointed officials responsible to them (e.g. district heads), kept control of the existing legal system and were responsible for collecting taxes, some of which were kept in the local treasury and some handed over to the central government. This method of rule was cheap and peaceful for the British, but it emphasised the conservative, static aspects of society and prevented progress.

Indirect rule in Igboland

The attempt to apply indirect rule among the Igbo of south-eastern Nigeria provides a good example of the failure of British attempts to rule segmentary societies indirectly. The Igbo lived in village groups with no chiefs. In order to rule indirectly the British created artificial chiefs, known as 'warrant chiefs'. They were not respected nor obeyed and the extent of their unpopularity was shown by the Women's Riots of 1929. Indirect rule methods were also strongly criticised by the rapidly expanding Igbo educated elite. During the 1930s the British made a careful study of Igbo society and eventually replaced indirect rule by a more democratic system.

The growth of nationalism

Some sort of nationalist feeling was present throughout the colonial period, at first with the idea of seeking constitutional reform, but rapidly becoming more radical until independence was demanded and won. Nationalism developed earlier and was stronger in British than in French West Africa, because of the presence of a larger educated elite and the greater freedom allowed. Both the First and the Second World Wars were turning-points in the development of nationalism.

Early nationalism in British West Africa

The earliest nationalist movements can be traced back to the nineteenth century in the small coastal colonies (e.g. the Aborigines Rights Protection Society founded in Ghana in 1897 to prevent the alienation of land). It was not, however, until after the First World War that nationalism emerged as a major force to be reckoned with. The National Congress of British West Africa, founded by Casely Hayford in 1918, held its main meeting in Accra in 1920 and was attended by representatives from all four British territories. The Congress passed eighty-three resolutions covering every aspect of colonial administration and later in the year sent a delegation to London to bring their grievances before the British Government. The Congress, not supported by the traditional rulers or the masses, and strongly criticised by the colonial authorities, achieved nothing immediately, the idea of a united British West Africa soon failed, and the Congress collapsed. It did, however, help to bring about concessions during the 1920s (e.g. constitutions with some representation and more Africans in the senior civil service), and it was an inspiration to later nationalist leaders.

During the 1920s and 1930s nationalist activities were restricted to the educated elite in the colony areas. Their demands were moderate (e.g. they wanted the number of Africans in the senior civil service increased and Africans in the legislative and executive councils. The educated elite were hostile to indirect rule and this produced conflict between them and the traditional rulers. The 1922 Clifford constitution in Nigeria provided for three elected and fifteen unofficial members of the legislative council and similar constitutions were obtained by Sierra Leone in 1924 and Ghana in 1925. British officials retained a majority and the Governor retained a veto, but the introduction of a limited elective element encouraged the growth of political parties (e.g. the Nigerian National Democratic Party founded by Herbert Macaulay in 1923).

Nationalism became more radical in the 1930s and the moderate leadership and limited aims of the educated elite began to be challenged. Tete-Ansa's 'West African Cooperative Producers Ltd' in Ghana and the 1937 Cocoa Hold-up showed the growing determination to resist economic exploitation. Youth movements were founded with more radical policies and wider support (e.g. the Nigerian Youth Movement founded in 1934 and the West African Youth League founded by Wallace Johnson in Sierra Leone in 1938). Throughout this period newspapers (e.g. the *Lagos Weekly Record* and the *Sierra Leone Weekly News*) played a major part in strengthening and spreading nationalist feeling. These early nationalists did important work in preparing the way for rapid progress towards independence after the Second World War.

Early nationalism in French West Africa

In French West Africa political parties, freedom of the press and criticism of colonial rule were allowed only in the four communes of Senegal. Elsewhere any type of political activity could, until the Second World War, lead to imprisonment without trial as happened to Hunkarin and his followers in Benin in the 1920s. Until 1946 the main aim of nationalists in the four communes was to get citizenship extended thereby freeing the people from such burdens as the 'in-digénat' and forced labour.

By far the most influential early nationalist leader was Blaise Diagne. In 1914 he became the first African to be elected to the French Chamber of Deputies by the four communes and until 1930 he and his party, the Republican Socialist Party, dominated Senegal politics. In 1916 he got a law passed (the 'Loi Diagne') which confirmed the citizenship rights of the inhabitants of the four communes, and in 1918 he helped the French recruit thousands of troops to fight in the First World War. In the 1920s his close cooperation with the French authorities made him increasingly unpopular and younger, more radical nationalists (e.g. Lamine Gueye) emerged.

There was much political activity in the four communes in the 1920s and 1930s centred around election to the municipal councils, the Colonial Council and the French Chamber of Deputies. This influenced the rest of French West Africa where politics were not allowed. The small elite were well-treated, but still opposition to assimilation developed (e.g. in the 1930s Senghor and other intellectuals developed the idea of 'Négritude' which emphasises the importance of African culture). By 1936 there were only about 80,000 African French citizens in the federation (78,000 of these in the four communes), and it was not until after the Second World War that nationalist politics could begin in all the territories of the federation.

The movement towards independence

By 1945 there was great demand for change, and also an able leadership to push for independence. It took West Africa only twenty years to win its independence: Ghana was the first to become independent in 1957 and most of the rest of West Africa followed suit in 1960. The Second World War greatly strengthened nationalism, and both the British and the French made constitutional reforms immediately after the war (e.g. the British granted new constitutions to Nigeria and Ghana in 1946, and in the same year the French extended citizenship to all Africans, abolished forced labour and the 'indigénat' and greatly extended representation).

Nationalist parties using modern political methods and appealing to the masses were formed, for example the National Council of Nigeria and the Cameroons (NCNC) led by Azikwe in Nigeria, the Convention People's Party (CPP) led by Nkrumah in Ghana, the Rassemblement Démocratique Africain (RDA) led by Houphouët-Boigny in French West Africa, and the Parti Africana Independencia para Guinea e Cabo Verde (PAIGC) led by Amilcar Cabral in Portuguese Guinea. Only in Portuguese Guinea was a war of liberation necessary: in the rest of West Africa, although there were some violent incidents in the late 1940s and early 1950s, fighting was avoided.

In British West Africa the main areas of dispute between the colonial authorities and the nationalist leaders concerned the speed at which independence should be granted and the role of the traditional rulers. In French West Africa few asked for full independence until the mid 1950s, and there was great disagreement between nationalist leaders about whether the federation should continue (supported by Senghor) or whether each territory should develop separately (supported by Houphouët-Boigny). In the British territories independence was gradually prepared for by a series of constitutional reforms during the 1950s, Africanising the government and increasing self-government. In French West Africa independence came more suddenly, the crucial turning-points being the 1956 'Loi Cadre' which abolished the federation and the 1958 referendum in which Guinea, led by Sekou Toure, voted for full independence.

Ghana was the first to achieve independence because of its large educated elite, rapid economic and social change (largely as a result of cocoa exports), its relatively small size and good communications, and the considerable unity preserved by the CPP under Nkrumah's able leadership. In Nigeria independence was delayed by strong regional feeling, as the support of each of the main political parties was based on one region, the NCNC on the east, the Action Group (AG) on the west, and the Northern Peoples' Congress (NPC) on the north.

Nationalism developed more slowly in French West Africa because of the smaller, better treated educated elite, the severe restrictions on political activity before 1946, representation in the National Assembly in Paris, and greater French determination to hang on to their colonies.

18

Central Africa c. 1900–60

For ease of study, huge, sparsely populated Central Africa is considered in four sections, the areas under French, Belgian, Portuguese and British control.

French Central Africa

This area comprises Cameroon (ruled by Germany until the First World War after which most of the country was mandated to France), the four territories of Chad, the Central African Republic (known as Ubangi-Chari during the colonial period), Gabon and Congo-Brazzaville (formerly French Congo) which were in 1910 joined into the Federation of French Equatorial Africa. The whole area ranging from dense forest in the south to desert in the north is sparsely populated (e.g. Gabon has a population density of two per square kilometre and Chad and the Central African Republic three per square kilometre). This small population, the lack of natural resources, and relative isolation meant very limited development (e.g. very few railways) during the colonial period. The French concentrated on their strategically more important territories in northern and western Africa and neglected equatorial Africa. In the nineteenth century the area had few trading links with Europe, and during the first decades of colonial rule ruthless exploitation was used in order to try to finance the colonial administration; to do this, large areas were leased out to trading companies.

The Federation, with the Governor-General at the federal capital of Brazzaville, was ruled in the same way as the Federation of French West Africa with much centralisation and administrative and economic assimilation. No political activity was allowed until after the Second World War, but the absence of a white settler community allowed relatively smooth progress towards independence which was achieved in 1960. Cameroon, which, as a League of Nations mandate territory, avoided the worst abuses of colonial rule, also achieved independence in 1960 and in 1961, as a result of a United Nations referendum, the southern part of the British West Cameroons was united to Cameroon while the northern part joined Nigeria.

Belgian Africa

Zaïre, the second largest country in Africa, entered the colonial period as the personal empire of King Leopold II (the Congo Free State), and in 1908 was taken over by the Belgian Government as the Belgian Congo. The small, densely populated countries of Rwanda and Burundi were ruled under mandate by Belgium after being taken from Germany during the First World War. In Zaïre there was fierce resistence to the establishment of Belgian rule (e.g. from the Azande led by Yambio 1892–1912) and frequent rebellions during the colonial period (e.g. the Bapende revolt in Kasai in 1921). In the early years of colonial rule, in order to raise money quickly, large areas of land and mineral rights were leased to concessionaire companies (e.g. the 'Compagnie du Katanga') and wild rubber was ruthlessly exploited.

Belgian rule was an extreme form of paternalism. With no other colonies, Belgium concentrated fully on Central Africa and rapid economic and social progress was made in such fields as primary education, health and communications. Belgian rule was, however, basically racialist and autocratic: no higher education was provided (at the time of independence in 1960 there were only thirty graduates), the people of Zaïre were given no role in government, little contact with the rest of Africa was allowed, and there was no freedom of the press or political association until 1959. Although political activity was strictly banned, opposition to Belgian rule showed itself in other ways, for example in support for religious movements such as Kimbanguism and Kitawala (see Chapter 15), and in strikes and riots. Zaïre, rich in natural resources, was provided with a good economic infrastructure, but there was less political preparation for independence than anywhere in Africa and this produced tragic results.

Because of Belgian restrictions nationalism developed very late: the first call for independence was made in 1956 by Joseph Kasuvubu, the leader of ABAKO, a Bakongo ethnic union. The whole movement towards independence was squeezed into the four years 1956–60. Economic depression, urban unemployment and Belgian divisions (e.g. a breakdown in cooperation between the colonial authorities, the Catholic church and the powerful companies) all contributed to the rapid changes in the late 1950s. Municipal government reforms in 1957 were the first Belgian concession, and the many ethnic unions soon developed into political parties in the main towns. In January 1959 serious rioting broke out in the capital Kinshasa (then called Leopoldville). The Belgian authorities called in troops, hundreds of rioters were killed, and law and order rapidly broke down throughout the country. The Belgians had no wish for a long colonial war and so began negotiating independence with the leaders of some of the new political parties. A disunited, unprepared Zaïre became independent in June 1960, with Joseph Kasuvubu as President and Patrice Lumumba as Prime Minister. A few days after independence the army mutinied, and Zaïre collapsed into chaos and civil war.

Belgium ruled the mandate territories of Rwanda and Burundi in much the same way as Zaïre. Both became independent in 1962, but there also there were serious problems, especially conflict between the two main ethnic groups, the Bahutu and the Watutsi.

Portuguese Central Africa

The Portuguese had been established on the coasts of Angola and Mozambique for many centuries. During the partition, the African peoples of the interior put up lengthy resistance to Portuguese control and throughout the colonial period there were frequent rebellions. Portugal's poverty and her authoritarian system of government made Portuguese rule both repressive and exploitative. During the Salazar dictatorship (1933–68), there was considerable white settlement in both territories (e.g. in Angola the white population rose from 30,000 in 1930 to 170,000 in 1960 and 250,000 in 1970). The mass of the African population were 'indigénas' with no rights at all, and less than half a per cent of the population (about 25,000 in Mozambique) ever became 'assimilado' with full citizenship rights.

There was very little economic and social development, a lot of land was given to companies to exploit and forced labour was used widely. Only in the last years of colonial rule was there much large-scale investment for major developments (e.g. the Cabora Bassa dam in Mozambique) and most of that came from countries other than Portugal. In 1951 both Angola and Mozambique were made 'overseas provinces' of Portugal, the growing trend towards independence in the rest of Africa was ignored, and the Portuguese were prepared to keep control at any cost. There were some reforms during the 1950s (e.g. the establishment of legislative councils in 1953 and an improvement in education), but Portuguese rule remained oppressive and very unpopular.

Nationalism developed rapidly in the 1950s, but any criticism of Portuguese rule was savagely repressed (e.g. in 1956 forty-six dockworkers were shot dead in Maputo). This repression forced nationalists to operate in secret and to use force as the only method of gaining freedom. Several nationalist parties were started in Angola, for example the Popular Front for the Liberation of Angola (MPLA) in 1956 and the National Union for the Total Independence of Angola (UNITA) in 1966, and in Mozambique the Mozambique Liberation Front (known as FRELIMO) began in 1962. The liberation war in Angola began in 1961 and in Mozambique in 1964. The Portuguese reacted by bringing in more troops, destroying villages, seeking help from South Africa, encouraging disunity and introducing belated reforms. Despite considerable disunity and the assassination of the FRELIMO leader, Eduardo Mondlane, in 1969, very rapid progress was made (e.g. FRELIMO opened a new front in the Tete area in 1972). Algeria was the only other part of Africa that had to fight as hard as the Portuguese territories to become independent. In 1974 a revolution changed the government in Portugal and in 1975 independence was granted to both Mozambique and Angola.

British Central Africa

Three British territories were created in Central Africa during the partition: Northern and Southern Rhodesia (now Zambia and Zimbabwe) were conquered for Britain by the British South Africa Company led by Cecil Rhodes, while Nyasaland (now Malawi) became British largely as a result of missionary activity in the area. In 1953 the three territories were joined together in the Central African Federation. This federation was dissolved in 1963, and Zambia and Malawi became independent in 1964, but in Zimbabwe the struggle for independence has only just ended. There were some white settlers in all three territories, but only in Zimbabwe were they strong enough to seize control, create a South African style society and delay majority rule.

Malawi

In Malawi missionary influence prevented company control and large-scale white settlement. Thanks to the missionaries, Malawi produced an educated elite earlier than neighbouring territories, but there was little economic development, so throughout the colonial period relatively-densely populated Malawi exported manpower both as migrant labour for the mines and as an influential educated elite. Independent churches were very important (e.g. John Chilembwe who led a rebellion in 1915 and the WatchTower movement). Several native associations (e.g. the North Nyasa Native Association) were created before 1920 and advocated limited reforms. Nationalism grew stronger in the 1920s and 1930s and found expression not only in the native associations but also in the many independent churches and in the district councils and native authorities which formed part of the indirect rule type of government. In 1944 the Nyasaland African Congress was founded and took the lead in opposing the creation of the federation in 1953. Hastings Banda became leader of the Congress in 1958, and independence was granted in 1964.

Zambia

Zambia, larger and more sparsely populated, had less educational development, greater mineral wealth and more problems with white settlers. The British South Africa Company gained control of Zambia in the 1890s, largely through treaty-making, and retained control until 1924 when the British Government took over. Only six per cent of the land was seized as Crown land to be leased to Europeans and white settlement was confined to small areas, especially along the central railway. Barotseland (as the British called the Lozi kingdom) managed during the partition to secure a special status and the Lozi chiefs retained considerable powers. During the period of company rule very little development took place, and Zambia was regarded largely as a source of labour for the mines and industries of Zimbabwe and South Africa.

During the early 1930s the rich copper reserves began to be exploited on a large scale (e.g. between 1930 and 1933 Zambia's exports, ninety per cent of which were copper, increased fivefold). Zambians got little benefit from the copper mining, but many moved to the copperbelt to work in the mines, and agricultural development was neglected. The British ruled Zambia by indirect rule methods in which little provision was made for the detribalised urban Africans of the copperbelt. In the 1930s there were about 15,000 white settlers, but by the time of Independence there were about 70,000 of them.

Nationalism developed rapidly in the 1930s: in 1935 the mineworkers went on strike for the first time, independent churches became influential and welfare associations were created in the towns. The first modern nationalist party, the Northern Rhodesia African National Congress, was founded in 1951, with Harry Nkumbala as President. It opposed the creation of the federation in 1953, fearing domination by the white settlers of Southern Rhodesia (Zimbabwe). Kenneth Kaunda emerged as the leader of the nationalist movement in the late 1950s and the nationalists succeeded in preventing white settler domination and getting the federation dissolved. Kaunda and the United National Independence Party led Zambia to independence in 1964.

Zimbabwe

The large white settler population has made the development of Zimbabwe unique, moving more and more towards the racialist South African pattern of a white monopoly of politics. The two main ethnic groups, the Ndebele and Shona, were subdued by the British South Africa Company in the early 1890s, and again after their great rebellion in 1896–97, and dispossessed of much of their best land. It took the Shona a long time to recover from these defeats, but the Ndebele 'indunas' retained some authority, and about 1920 Lobengula's son, Nyamanda, led a campaign for the revival of the Ndebele kingship and for a Ndebele national home.

In 1923 Company rule ended and Zimbabwe became a British colony, but the 1923 constitution gave the small white population almost complete freedom to govern as they wished. The white settler population increased rapidly from 48,000 in 1930 to over 200,000 in 1960. Throughout the colonial period African grievances centred on the loss of land, as the 1930 Land Apportionment Act assigned fifty per cent of the best land to the white settlers.

As the white settlers consolidated their position of dominance, nationalism developed. In 1923 the Rhodesian Bantu Voters Association was formed, initially mostly with leaders from Malawi and South Africa because of the lack of educational facilities in Zimbabwe. In the 1930s, Ndebele and Shona took the lead in the growing nationalist movement, trade-unionism developed, and independent churches became important.

Nationalist activity increased after the Second World War, and in 1948 there was a general strike. In the early 1950s the white settlers were in favour of the federation, hoping that through it they would extend their influence, consolidate their dominance and gain economically. Africans were at first divided in their attitude to the federation, but most soon realised that all talk of racial partnership was hypocrisy and that the settlers were determined to strengthen their control. In 1957 a more radical Southern Rhodesia African National Congress was revived under the leadership of Joshua Nkomo, but was soon banned. As the white minority government became more repressive, nationalism was forced to become more radical. The Zimbabwe African Peoples Union was formed in 1962 under the leadership of Nkomo and Sithole: it was soon banned and in 1963 Nkomo and Sithole formed separate rival parties. In 1965 the white minority government, led by Ian Smith, unilaterally declared independence from Britain. After that the nationalist struggle continued and a war of liberation developed. Finally, in April 1980, a majority government was elected, Mugabe became Prime Minister and Zimbabwe gained legal independence.

19

East Africa c. 1900–60

During the partition Uganda, Kenya and Zanzibar were acquired by the British, while Tanganyika (now united with Zanzibar and known as Tanzania) was acquired by the Germans. After the First World War Tanganyika became a British mandate territory, and so from 1919 the whole area was ruled by Britain. During the 1920s there was a lot of discussion about creating some sort of East African union (e.g. the 1929 Ormsby-Gore Commission and the 1928 Hilton-Young Commission). The idea was eventually dropped because of opposition from all groups except the Kenyan white settlers. Union was opposed by the Baganda who wanted to preserve their special position; by most Africans in all three territories who feared white Kenyan domination; by Governor Cameron of Tanganyika who wanted to preserve Tanganyika's special mandate status; and by the white settlers in Uganda and Tanganyika who did not wish to be dominated by the more numerous white settlers in Kenya.

From 1930 there were regular meetings of governors to coordinate economic and social matters and in 1948 an East African Commission with headquarters in Nairobi was established and did much valuable coordinating work (e.g. in railways, posts, defence and higher education). The small number of educated Africans and settler influence, especially in Kenya, delayed the development of nationalism in East Africa. There was little nationalist activity until after the Second World War.

Uganda

To make their occupation effective and to facilitate economic exploitation, it was essential for the British to improve communications between Uganda and the coast. Between 1896 and 1901 a railway was constructed from Mombasa on the coast to Kisumu on Lake Victoria: although this was always known as the Uganda railway, it was not extended actually into Uganda until the 1930s.

The Buganda Agreement

In 1899 Sir Harry Johnstone was sent by the British to Uganda as special commissioner to organise effective British administration. Johnstone realised that the cooperation of the leaders of the powerful kingdom of Buganda was essential. After lengthy discussions with the Baganda leaders, especially the 'katikiro' (chief minister) Sir Apolo Kagwa, the Buganda Agreement was signed in 1900. This agreement controlled relations between the British and Buganda throughout the colonial period and was important in three main areas.

a) Land. The boundaries of Buganda were defined (including recent conquests from Bunyoro) and a system of freehold land tenure was introduced. About half the land, known as 'mailo' land, was assigned to the kabaka, his ministers and chiefs, causing grievances later on from those left out, for example the Bataka chiefs (clan-heads).

b) Government. The traditional Baganda system of government (e.g. the kabaka and lukiko) was retained. The Buganda Government was given considerable control over its own affairs and this was later to cause frequent conflict between the Buganda Government and the British protectorate government.

c) Tax. The Buganda Government was to hand over to the protectorate government all revenue collected, but in return for this no further taxes were to be imposed without the consent of the kabaka and lukiko.

This agreement meant greater powers to the chiefs and the ministers and less power to the kabaka and the Bataka clan-heads. Similar agreements, but with less power kept by the traditional governments, were signed with the smaller kingdoms of Toro in 1900 and Nkore in 1901.

British rule

The British made much use of Baganda officials and methods to extend their control (e.g. in the early years of the twentieth century, Semei Kakungulu spread British rule and Baganda methods to Teso, Lango and Busoga). It took the British many years to establish full control in the northern areas, and throughout the protectorate the British used indirect rule methods as much as possible. In 1902 a large part of eastern Uganda was transferred to Kenya.

Early on there was great emphasis on the development of cash crops and, largely as a result of the influence of Governor Hesketh Bell, Uganda developed with an economy based on peasant agriculture rather than on European plantations. The growing of cotton was begun in 1904 and by 1914 cotton was the major export. During the first two decades of colonial rule Sir Apolo Kagwa, katikiro and regent for the young kabaka Daudi Chwa, was very influential and did much to encourage both agriculture and education.

From about 1920 onwards there was almost constant conflict between the British protectorate government, the Buganda Government and the kabaka (e.g. rivalry between Kagwa and the kabaka led to Kagwa's resignation in 1926, and the Bataka clan-heads struggled for land). Buganda's virtual autonomy under the kabaka delayed the development of any sense of national unity.

Nationalism

The nationalist movement in Uganda was very divided and this delayed independence: the Baganda leaders were determined to maintain Buganda's privileged position; nationalism was moderate in the other kingdoms and more radical in the rest of the protectorate. The first Africans joined the legislative council in 1945 and the number of Africans was increased in 1949. In 1949 there was serious rioting against both the Buganda Government and the British Government. The Baganda were suspicious of any constitutional developments which they felt might weaken their own special position and in 1953 relations between the British Government and the Buganda Government broke down completely. This produced a major crisis during which the kabaka, Mutesa II, was exiled: all the Baganda united to demand the kabaka's return and he was restored in 1955.

The first modern political party, the Uganda National Congress, was founded in 1952, but was opposed by most of the Baganda leaders. In 1956 the Democratic Party was founded with largely Baganda Catholic support under the leadership of Benedict Kiwanuka. After the 1958 elections some UNC members and independents combined to form the Uganda Peoples' Congress under the leadership of Milton Obote, and this party soon replaced the UNC as the leading non-Baganda party. In the 1961 elections, the Democratic Party gained a small majority over the UPC and in the same year important constitutional concessions were made to Buganda. In March 1962 Uganda gained internal self-government with Kiwanuka as Prime Minister, and in October 1962 full independence under the leadership of Milton Obote heading an alliance of the UPC and the Baganda 'Kabaka Yekka' party.

Kenya

The establishment of British rule

In the late nineteenth century Kenya was regarded by the British as little more than a route to Uganda. The British sent few administrative officials, and few Kenyan societies had strong centralised governments, so the establishment of an effective administration was a slow process. The British made use of and strengthened the chiefs (e.g. Mumia of Wanga) wherever possible. The British gained control of the Maasai through two agreements (both of which they later broke) with Lenana, the Maasai laibon, in 1904 and 1911. Most of the peoples of Kenya resisted British conquest as strongly as possible (e.g. the Nandi and the Embu).

In the first years of the twentieth century white settlement began especially in the fertile highlands around Nairobi which soon became known as the 'white highlands'. In 1907 the capital was moved from Mombasa to Nairobi and a legislative council was established. Gradually the whole territory was divided into provinces and districts under provincial and district commissioners, and financial self-sufficiency was soon achieved as a result of coffee exports.

Inter-war settler problems

The number of white settlers in Kenya grew rapidly and by the 1940s there were over 30,000. During the first two decades of the century the settlers, led by Lord Delamere, became very influential, and there was frequent conflict between the settlers and the British Government over land and labour. During the same period a large, urban, trading Indian community settled in Kenya. Settler determination to control the land and to obtain cheap African labour made Kenya's history the most troubled in East Africa during the inter-war period.

The settlers became most powerful in the years immediately following the First World War.

115

a) White settlers were given seats on the executive council in 1918.
b) The Northey Circular in 1919 was the nearest the settlers got to government support for the control of African labour.
c) In 1920 all Africans were forced to carry an identity card, the 'kipande'.

The settlers wanted to became a self-governing dominion under white control and around 1920 it seemed that Kenya, like Zimbabwe, would develop into a racialist society ruled by the white minority. In the 1920s, however, the British began to be more aware of their responsibilities towards the African population. The 1923 Devonshire White Paper stated quite clearly that 'Primarily Kenya is an African country and the interests of the African natives must be paramount'. Basically the British were saying that there would be no further advance towards self-government under white rule. Throughout the 1920s and 1930s the main theme of Kenya's politics was the relationship between the various racial groups: white settlers, Indians and Africans. Little was done to encourage the development of African agriculture, since the settlers preferred the Africans to remain as a supply of cheap labour for their plantations. The Africans, especially the Kikuyu (the largest group in Kenya), had lost much of their best land to the white settlers, and the rapidly growing population meant increasing land hunger and discontent.

Nationalism

Nationalism began earlier in Kenya, especially among the Kikuyu, than in the rest of East Africa. Harry Thuku founded the Young Kikuyu Association in 1922 and this later developed into the Kikuyu Central Association. During the 1930s anti-European feeling increased, there was strong Kikuyu opposition to missionary attempts to ban female circumcision, and many independent Kikuyu schools were started. Also in the late 1930s nationalism began among other groups (e.g. the Luo and Kavirondo). In 1944 Eliud Mathu became the first African on the legislative council and in the same year the Kenyan African Union was founded, the leadership of which was taken over by Jomo Kenyatta in 1947.

So bad did conditions become after the Second World War, especially for the Kikuyu who had lost their land, that violence broke out in 1952. This violence in the Central and Rift Valley provinces is known as Mau Mau, and a brutal guerrilla war continued till 1955. Only ninety-five Europeans were killed, but about 13,000 Africans lost their lives during the Mau Mau troubles. The outbreak of violence led the British to declare a state of emergency and to introduce reforms (e.g. more Africans were appointed to the civil service, a new land distribution scheme was introduced, and rapid constitutional advances were made – the Lyttleton constitution 1954 is an example). Mau Mau was important not only because of these reforms but also because it showed the white settlers that Kenya must develop as an African-controlled country.

Because of the state of emergency, no politics at national level were allowed throughout the 1950s and this delayed the emergence of mass political parties. During this period the trade unions were important, especially the Kenya Federation of Labour whose general secretary was Tom Mboya. Kenyatta, who was unjustly imprisoned as a result of Mau Mau, remained the most significant nationalist leader. In 1960 two national parties were formed, the Kenya African

National Union (KANU) and the Kenya African Democratic Union (KADU). Decisive constitutional steps were made in 1960 when the Macleod constitution provided for a common electoral roll and an African majority on the legislative council. Ethnic rivalries delayed independence till 1963, when Kenya became independent under Kenyatta.

Tanzania

German rule

The German Government took over control of Tanganyika from the German East Africa Company in 1889 as a result of the Abushiri rebellion. It took the Germans the whole period until the First World War to establish firm control throughout the territory, and German rule, at least in the early years, was brutal. The whole country was divided into districts and the District Officers were given great powers. Wherever possible, use was made of chiefs, but where there were no chiefs, coastal Arabs or Swahili were used as agents, known as 'akida'. There was some economic progress (e.g. the building of railways and the development of sisal as the main export crop) and by 1913 there were 5,000 white settlers.

The Maji Maji War (1905–07) was the last and most serious rebellion against German rule. It was a reaction to the brutality of German rule and its immediate cause was a German attempt to force the growing of cotton. It began in 1905 with the teaching of the traditional religious leader, Kinjikitile, and spread rapidly from the Rufiji area until most of the peoples of southern Tanganyika united in revolt. The Germans were taken by surprise and had to call in reinforcements. The rebellion was not finally crushed until January 1907 and during its suppression nearly 100,000 Africans died. The Maji Maji rebellion produced widescale devastation and death, but it also forced the Germans to moderate their policies.

From the time Rechenberg was appointed Governor in 1906, German rule was less brutal and more concerned with African needs. Sisal production expanded greatly, the growing of coffee became important in the Kilimanjaro and Bukoba areas, the education became more widespread. There was fighting in Tanganyika throughout the First World War and much death and destruction was caused. In 1919 Tanganyika became a League of Nations mandate territory under the British.

British rule

The British had a very difficult task in the early 1920s trying to repair the damage done during the First World War. The most important British Governor of Tanganyika was Cameron, Governor from 1925 to 1931. He had worked under Lugard in northern Nigeria and was determined to use indirect rule methods in Tanganyika despite the lack of large centralised states. His system of indirect administration was established by the Native Authority Ordinance of 1926, and during the following years councils of chiefs were established as local authorities (e.g. among the Sukuma and Nyamwezi). A stable, lasting local government system was achieved, but little was done to promote progress in other fields or national unity, and Tanganyika remained poor. The number of white settlers remained small and the British managed to resist settler demands for land and cheap labour, so that racial bitterness like that in Kenya never developed.

Nationalism

Despite its educational and economic backwardness, Tanganyika was the first state in East Africa to gain independence. Nationalism was helped by the absence of any one dominant ethnic group and by the use of the Swahili language throughout the country. The British were under pressure from the United Nations to introduce constitutional reform: they had hoped that the traditional rulers would emerge as the leaders of the independence movement, but by the mid 1950s it was clear that the educated elite were the nationalist leaders.

In 1954 the Tanganyika African National Union (TANU) was founded by Julius Nyerere as a very efficient mass political party. Nyerere convinced the white settlers that they had nothing to fear and in the elections to the legislative council in the late 1950s TANU won almost all seats. The British were anxious to avoid problems like those in the neighbouring states (Mau Mau and the kabaka crisis) and so Tanganyika moved smoothly and rapidly to independence, which was granted in 1961.

Zanzibar during the colonial period was ruled by the British indirectly through the sultan. It gained independence in 1963 but was very unstable: the sultan's government was overthrown in 1964 and Zanzibar united with Tanganyika to form Tanzania.

20

Twentieth-century southern Africa

For the rest of Africa, the Republic of South Africa remains a symbol of racial oppression. It is the only part of Africa still under white minority rule with little hope of freedom for the non-whites without a long armed struggle. Britain handed over control of South Africa to the white settlers in 1910 and since then, and especially since 1948, Boer ideas of racial separation (apartheid) and white domination have become more and more firmly established. The white settler community (under four million out of a total population of about twenty-five million) are determined to hang on to their privileged position. They have created the most ruthless police state in the world, and the achievement of independence in the rest of Africa during the last quarter of a century has only made the South African whites more determined to retain their supremacy.

Twentieth-century developments in the neighbouring territories of Namibia (formerly South-west Africa), Botswana (formerly Bechuanaland), Lesotho (formerly Basutoland) and Swaziland will also be briefly considered in this chapter.

South Africa from the Boer War to the Act of Union

During the Boer War (1899–1902) 80,000 Boers fought against half a million British troops and there was much cruelty on both sides. Neither side armed any Africans because both feared rebellion and so the war was entirely a war between two white communities. In 1900 the British captured the Boer capitals of Bloemfontain and Pretoria, and from then on the Boer leaders (e.g. Smuts and Botha) fought a guerrilla war, against which the British used scorched earth tactics and concentration camps. The war finally ended in 1902 with the Peace of Vereeniging, and the following were the main terms.
a) The Transvaal and the Orange Free State were to become British colonies.
b) Britain was to help repair war damage.
c) Responsible government for the colonies was promised for the near future.
d) The Afrikaans and English languages would have equal status.

At Vereeniging the British were trying to conciliate the Boers and so did nothing to help the African majority.

Boer parties (e.g. 'Het Volk' in the Transvaal) won the elections in both the Orange Free State and the Transvaal when they were granted responsible government in 1907. In 1908 the largely Boer South Africa Party won the elections in the Cape, so that Boers were then in control of all the colonies except Natal. During these years rapid moves were made towards the creation of a united South Africa.

These moves towards union were successful for many reasons.

a) All four colonies were organised in a similar way as British colonies.

b) Railway rivalry was reduced and greater economic unity was provided by the creation of a customs union.

c) Many wanted union in order to promote development and prevent war in the future.

d) The 1906 Bambata rebellion in Natal raised problems which could be more easily treated by a union.

A National Convention was held in 1908–09 to consider union and the main argument was between Boer racialists and those with more liberal attitudes from the Cape (the Cape allowed a few non-whites the right to vote). The needs and demands of the Africans were completely ignored by both white politicians in South Africa and the British Government. Compromise was reached, almost entirely in favour of Boer ideas, and in May 1910 the Union of South Africa Act came into force.

The main provisions of the Act of Union were.

a) The four colonies were to become four provinces in the Union of South Africa which was to be a self-governing colony.

b) The constitution was to be unitary rather than federal.

c) English and Dutch were to be joint languages.

d) Pretoria, Cape Town and Bloemfontain were to be joint capitals.

e) Only whites could be elected to parliament.

f) Each of the four provinces was to keep its existing franchise system (so the only non-whites to be allowed to vote would be the few qualified Coloureds and Africans in the Cape).

g) Greater voting weight was given to the rural areas, thus favouring the Boer rather than the English population.

h) Any part of the Act could be changed by a fifty per cent majority of the parliament, except the franchise and language clauses which needed a two-thirds majority to be changed.

Thus Britain totally abandoned her responsibilities for South Africa's non-whites, keeping control only of the three High Commission territories (present-day Botswana, Lesotho and Swaziland).

Political developments

Rivalry between the British and the Boers continued to be a major issue after the Act of Union. Until 1934 the Union was a self-governing colony; in 1934 it became fully independent, and in 1961 it left the British Commonwealth and became a republic.

Governments since 1910

a) 1910–24 South Africa Party Government. During these years the largely Boer South Africa Party, led by Botha (1910–19) and Smuts (1919–24), tried to rule as a British-Boer partnership. The main opposition was provided by the extreme Afrikaner Nationalist Party led by Hertzog. During the First

World War South Africa fought on the British side but extremist Afrikaner republicans (e.g. de Wet) opposed participation in the war. After the First World War great problems were caused by job-rivalry in the cities between the 'poor whites' and the Africans, culminating in the 1922 Rand general strike which was ruthlessly suppressed by Smuts.

b) 1924–33 Pact Government. In 1924 the Nationalists led by Herzog gained power (with Labour support), and many racialist laws in support of the 'poor whites' were passed. The great depression of the early 1930s weakened this government and in 1933 an alliance was formed between Smuts's South Africa Party and Hertzog's Nationalists to create the United Party.

c) 1933–48 United Party Government. The United Party, led by Hertzog until 1939 and then by Smuts, ruled with the extreme Purified Nationalists, led by Malan, in opposition. During these years extreme Afrikaner feeling became increasingly influential (e.g. from the 'Ossendabrandwag' – Ox-wagon Sentinel – and the secret society known as the 'Broederband'). Much racialist legislation was passed in the 1930s. In 1939 Hertzog left the United Party in opposition to South Africa's support for Britain in the Second World War.

d) 1948 onwards Nationalist Party Government. The victory of Malan and the extreme Nationalists in 1948 was a turning-point in South African history: since then South Africa has been increasingly dominated by the Nationalist Party with its policy of racial discrimination known as apartheid. Malan was Prime Minister until 1954, and he was followed by Strydom, Verwoerd, Vorster and Botha. Legislation in the early 1950s greatly increased discrimination against non-whites in all fields and introduced full-scale apartheid. Despite criticism of apartheid from both inside and outside South Africa, Nationalist Party support has increased (e.g. in the 1977 elections the Nationalists won eighty-one per cent of the seats).

Apartheid

Since the 1910 Act of Union a series of laws has been passed discriminating against non-whites politically, economically and socially (e.g. land ownership, employment, education). By the time the Nationalist Party gained power in 1948, the non-whites were already treated as second-class citizens with virtually no rights. The Nationalists consolidated and extended this discriminatory legislation into the overall policy of apartheid. Apartheid has caused the non-whites much upheaval, suffering and humiliation, and has created a vicious circle of fear, of opposition to apartheid, and then of more extreme apartheid legislation. Apartheid is the twentieth-century culmination of the long-established racialism of the Boers (see Chapter 10).

From the great mass of apartheid legislation, the following may be selected as being the most important stages in its introduction.

a) Land. During the nineteenth-century expansion of white control, the Africans had been deprived of much of the best land. This was confirmed by the 1913 Land Act which introduced territorial segregation wholly in favour of the whites; Africans being restricted to a few small reserves. The 1936 Native Trusts and Lands Act took this process further, and only thirteen per cent of the land was left to the Africans who formed the vast majority of the population. In the 1950s apartheid land policies culminated in the idea of Bantustans: the 1959 Promotion of the Bantu Self-Government Act provided for the creation of semi-autonomous tribal African homelands known as Bantustans. The first to be created was the predominately Xhosa Transkei which was given a degree of self-government under Chief Minister Kaiser Matanzima in 1963 and so-called independence in 1976, the white government of the Republic retaining a veto on legislation and control of the military, police, posts, railways, customs and foreign affairs. The Bantustans are not in any real sense independent and the idea of Bantustans is totally impractical for the following reasons.

- The Bantustans cannot survive economically: they are small, fragmented and overcrowded, with poor soil, no resources and little investment. They can never support the large, rapidly-growing African population.
- The Bantustan policy makes no provision for the Coloured and Indian populations.
- The African urban population now numbers about ten million: they are integrated into the economy of the supposedly white areas and the South African economy is dependent on their labour.

b) Employment. The 1911 Mines and Works Act and the 1926 Colour Bar Act restricted Africans to unskilled work and low wages. The 1924 Industrial Conciliation Act banned African trade unions and the 1923 Native (Urban Areas) Act, reinforced by later amendments, introduced strict control of Africans in the towns and created a contract labour force temporarily resident in the towns without their families. These measures deprived the Africans of a share in the rapid economic development and wealth their labour made possible.

c) Politics. The very limited African and Coloured voting rights in the Cape were removed by a series of measures beginning with the 1936 Representation of Natives Act and culminating in the 1959 Bantu Self-Government Act which removed all African representation and confined African political rights entirely to the Bantustans. The 1950 Suppression of Communism Act gave the government huge powers to suppress any criticism ruthlessly.

d) Education. One of the most extreme and inhuman aspects of apartheid can be seen in education. Education for non-whites was always neglected and much inferior to that provided for whites. The 1953 Bantu Education Act created a quite distinct system of 'education' (more correctly indoctrination) for the Africans in which they would be prepared from childhood for inequality and limited opportunities. The 1959 Extension of University Education Act introduced racial segregation at the university level.

e) Social restrictions. The 1949 Prohibition of Mixed Marriages Act banned interracial marriage and the 1950 Immorality (Amendment) Act extended this ban to any form of sexual relations. Pass laws restricting the movement of Africans developed in the nineteenth century and were continued and formalised in the twentieth century (e.g. an African could not leave his village without permission).

Opposition to apartheid, both inside and outside South Africa, continues to grow.

Economic development

South Africa is exceptionally rich in natural resources and this, together with white settler domination, has led to the growth of an economy different from that in the rest of Africa. The following were among the most important twentieth-century economic developments.

a) Mining. South Africa's economy has remained closely linked with mining, especially the mining of gold in the Witwatersrand area (South Africa produces seventy per cent of the world's gold) and diamonds in the Kimberley area. South Africa also possesses rich deposits of other minerals (e.g. uranium and coal).

b) Industry. Rapid industrialisation has taken place during the last half century in the Rand area and around the main seaports. Manufactured goods, which accounted for only three per cent of exports in 1939, provided forty per cent of exports in 1966.

c) Agriculture. Rapid agricultural development has also taken place, but only on white-owned lands. African agriculture on the poor soils of the thirteen per cent of the land assigned to Africans has been neglected, and agricultural production has not even kept up with the rise in population, so many Africans have to abandon farming and move to the towns.

d) Urbanisation. There has been rapid urbanisation (e.g. by 1936 forty-five per cent of the population lived in the nine largest cities). About half South Africa's white population now live in the Rand industrial-mining area in and around Johannesburg, and about ten million Africans are urban contract workers.

e) Labour. The development of both mining and industry has greatly increased the demand for African migrant labour. A two-tier labour system has developed with skilled and semi-skilled jobs reserved for the whites, and much lower wages are paid to African workers. There was strict racialist segregation in mining and industry long before apartheid became the official policy of the government and the very considerable wealth of South Africa remains concentrated in the hands of the dominant white minority.

Nationalism

In 1912 the South African National Congress (later simply called the African National Congress – ANC) was formed and during the next decades tried by means of protests, petitions and delegations to improve African conditions. Little was achieved by the ANC and during the 1920s and 1930s the Industrial and Commercial Workers Union of Africa (ICU), founded by Clements Kadalie in 1921 and claiming a membership of 200,000 by 1928, was more influential.

During the late 1940s the ANC was reorganised and strengthened, and the ANC Youth League, which demanded stronger action, soon took over the leadership. In 1949–50 there were large-scale strikes and riots and in 1952 a Defiance Campaign was led against some of the worst aspects of segregation. The Congress of the People was formed in 1955 and linked Africans, Indians and Coloureds in protest against apartheid, but most of the leaders were arrested before much could be achieved. During the 1950s the ANC under Luthuli's leadership was in favour of moderate, peaceful methods, and this produced a split in 1958 when Robert Sobukwe founded the more radical Pan African Congress (PAC).

During a campaign against the Pass Laws in 1960, over two hundred unarmed Africans were massacred at Sharpeville, and in 1961 both the ANC and the PAC were banned. By then the white minority government was so repressive against any form of opposition that nationalist activity had to continue in secret (e.g. the 'Umkanto We Sizwe' – 'Spear of the Nation' – founded by Nelson Mandela in 1961). Thousands of Africans have been imprisoned, often without trial, and many have had to flee into exile. Despite the severity of repression, African opposition to the evils of apartheid and African desire for majority rule has continued (e.g. the Soweto riots of 1976).

Other states

The former High Commission territories

Swaziland, Lesotho and Botswana avoided white settler domination. Britain used indirect rule methods and did very little to develop them, so they have remained economically very dependent on South Africa (e.g. half the adult male population of Lesotho, a small mountainous country completely surrounded by South Africa, work as migrant labourers in South Africa). During the 1950s and 1960s, the three states developed peacefully and constitutionally towards independence, Botswana becoming independent in 1966 led by Seretse Khama, Lesotho also in 1966 led by Chief Jonathan, and Swaziland in 1968 led by King Sobhuza II.

Namibia

Very large but sparsely-populated Namibia became a German colony in 1884. Brutal German rule greatly reduced the population (composed largely of Ovambo, Herero and Nama). In 1920 Namibia became a South African mandate territory, and since then there has been a great increase in white settlers (now about 90,000 in a population of 750,000) and growing South African exploitation and oppression.

During the last twenty years three main developments have occurred.
a) There has been considerable international debate about the legal position of Namibia as a United Nations trust territory. In 1966 the United Nations cancelled South Africa's mandate and in 1971 the International Court ordered South Africa to free Namibia.
b) Apartheid has been increasingly introduced, Africans being regarded as cheap migrant labour and provision being made for the creation of six Bantustans.
c) African nationalism has grown rapidly. Hosea Kutako, the Paramount Chief of the Herero (1917–70), became a symbol of early nationalism and did much to bring Namibian problems to world attention. In 1960 the South West African Peoples Organisation (SWAPO) was founded by Sam Nujama to fight for Namibian freedom.

South Africa has illegally kept control of Namibia as long as possible partly because of the country's great mineral resources, especially diamonds, and partly as a buffer between itself and independent black Africa. At last steps are being taken to grant independence, but not to SWAPO, the nationalist movement officially recognised by the United Nations and the Organisation of African Unity.

21

Nationalism and the achievement of independence

Like Chapters 13–15, this is a general chapter: it will deal with the aspects of the nationalist struggle for independence which affected most of Africa, especially the causes for the growth of nationalism, and the importance of the Second World War. In a European context, nationalism usually implies common race, language, culture and history, none of which existed in colonial Africa. African nationalism can be defined as a feeling of national consciousness, an awareness by people that they are members of a nation-state, and a desire for freedom from colonial rule.

General points

Nationalism varied considerably: the character which it took and the speed at which it developed depended on the African background (e.g. in North Africa Islam contributed to nationalism) and on the policies of the colonial rulers (e.g. the British allowed greater freedom and were more ready to give up their colonies than the Portuguese). Where there were a large number of white settlers, land was a crucial issue and the determination of the settlers to retain control usually forced the nationalist movement to turn to violence (e.g. in Algeria, Kenya, Angola, Zimbabwe). Generally nationalism developed earlier in North Africa than in Africa south of the Sahara.

Despite these variations, it is possible to distinguish three main phases in the development of nationalism.

a) 1890–1920. During these decades nationalism usually took the form of rural uprisings (e.g. the Shona-Ndebele rebellion of 1896–97 and the Maji Maji rebellion of 1905–07). Only in the coastal cities of British West Africa and in North Africa was there a large-enough educated elite to criticise colonial rule. The growth of independent church movements (e.g. the Chilembwe rebellion in Malawi in 1915) can also be regarded as an early expression of nationalist feeling.

b) 1920s and 1930s. The period between the First and the Second World War was a period of increasing education and urbanisation, both of which encouraged the growth of nationalism. External influences, especially from black Americans and from Africans studying abroad, became important. Nationalism was generally more developed in West Africa than in East and Central Africa, and in British Africa than in French Africa. It was moderate and was confined to a small urban educated elite. In much of Africa, especially in the Belgian and the Portuguese territories, repressive colonial policies prevented the early growth of nationalism.

c) 1945 onwards. The third and final phase of nationalism began immediately after the Second World War with the emergence of new leaders, new parties, newspapers, trade unions and demands for rapid progress towards independence. The process of decolonisation was very rapid and often independence was granted with little preparation. The varying strengths of the nationalist movements and the varying determination of the colonial powers to retain control can be seen from the different dates at which parts of Africa achieved independence. (See Map 13.)

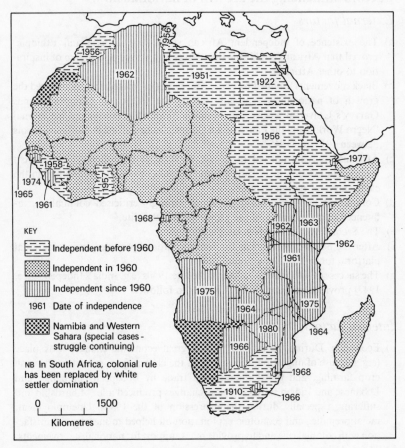

KEY

[▦] Independent before 1960

[▨] Independent in 1960

[▥] Independent since 1960

1961 Date of independence

[▩] Namibia and Western Sahara (special cases - struggle continuing)

NB In South Africa, colonial rule has been replaced by white settler domination

0 ___ 1500

Kilometres

Map 13 Africa: the spread of independence

- Most of northern Africa (e.g. Morocco, Tunisia and Sudan) achieved independence in the mid 1950s, only Algeria having to fight until 1962.
- In the period 1957–60, most of British West Africa, French Africa and Zaïre gained independence. In 1960 no less than sixteen African countries were granted independence.

- During the early and mid 1960s independence came to British Central and East Africa (e.g. Zambia, Kenya).
- The Portuguese territories (Angola, Mozambique and Guinea-Bissau) gained their independence after a long struggle in 1974–5.
- Now Zimbabwe has gained independence (1980) and Namibia is moving towards it, leaving only South Africa as a continuing stronghold of white minority domination.

Factors influencing the growth of nationalism

External factors

a) The existence of independent African states (e.g. Liberia and Ethiopia) proved that Africans could rule themselves and served as a source of inspiration to other Africans.

b) Black movements founded by black Americans promoted and encouraged the growth of nationalism especially during the 1920s, for example Marcus Garvey's Universal Negro Improvement Association (UNIA) and his journal 'Negro World', and the Pan-African Congresses organised by William Dubois between 1919 and 1945.

c) Africans studying abroad (e.g. The West African Students Union WASU founded in London in 1925 by Ladipo Solanke) were often influential in the early stages of nationalism.

d) Communist and socialist ideas, which strongly criticised colonialism, influenced many members of the growing educated elite.

e) The Second World War (see later section).

f) After the Second World War the United Nations provided an international platform for criticism of colonial rule.

g) The success of nationalists in Asia in the late 1940s (e.g. India's Independence, 1947) provided an example for Africans to follow.

Internal factors

a) Economic. During the colonial period great economic changes took place (e.g. because of migration, urbanisation, the change from subsistence to cash crop farming, and the domination of trade by European companies and Lebanese and Indian traders). These changes produced a lot of hardship and suffering, especially during the depression of the 1930s. Unemployment, racial prejudice and economic exploitation all helped to increase dissatisfaction with colonial rule and to provide mass support for nationalist movements.

b) Social. Urbanisation weakened family and tribal ties, and improved communications helped to unite countries and to develop a sense of nationhood. By far the most important social cause, however, was the growth of European-style education. This produced leaders for the nationalist movement and provided them with a common language, and with new ideas and aspirations. Wherever education was most developed, nationalism was strongest.

c) Religious. To some extent nationalism was a reaction to the attempts of the early missionaries to destroy African culture. Moreover Christianity stressed the equality of all men, and in many parts of Africa the nationalist leaders were products of mission schools.

d) Political. During the partition states were created by grouping different tribal groups together, and during the colonial period common administration, language, trade and law gave these states some feeling of unity. The speed at which nationalism developed depended greatly on the degree of freedom allowed by the colonial power in such matters as press and political activity.

The importance of the Second World War

The Second World War (1939–45) affected Africa in many ways, all of which greatly assisted the growth of nationalism. The following were among the most important effects of the Second World War on Africa.

a) Africa was strategically and economically very important during the war, and Africa made a major contribution to the eventual victory of Britain, France and America over Germany. There was a lot of fighting in North Africa, and West and East Africa were vital as staging posts for getting troops and supplies to the Asian war-zone. The Japanese conquest of South-east Asia made Britain and France economically more dependent on Africa for raw materials (e.g. rubber, tin). In return for this assistance, both Britain and France promised reforms, and at the end of the war many of the worst features of colonial rule were abolished (e.g. the 'indigénat' in French-controlled Africa), and several new constitutions were introduced (e.g. in Ghana and Nigeria), providing for more African participation in government.

b) There was considerable economic prosperity during the war: exports of raw materials increased, many basic industries were started and there was greater government intervention in economic affairs. At the end of the war there was an economic depression which produced serious problems (e.g. unemployment in the cities). Also after the war most of the colonial powers introduced economic reforms (e.g. development plans and financial aid).

c) Many thousands of Africans were recruited into European armies (e.g. over 100,000 were recruited from West Africa by the French in 1943–44) and were sent to fight in Ethiopia, North Africa, Italy and Burma. They returned home after the war with new ideas and attitudes: they had served with, and fought against, ordinary white soldiers, who, they realised, were very similar to themselves, so the myth of white superiority was completely destroyed; they had experienced higher standards of living in other parts of the world and were therefore unwilling to accept existing conditions in Africa. Ex-soldiers played a major part in radical politics after the war.

d) During the war Britain and France were fighting to save themselves from German domination, and in their wartime propaganda they stressed the need for freedom (e.g. in the 1941 Atlantic Charter between Britain and America).

e) The war established the USSR and the USA as the most powerful nations in the world. For different reasons both these superpowers criticised European colonialism and put pressure on their European allies to disband their empires quickly. The European colonial powers emerged from the war economically exhausted and no longer first-class world powers. Britain and France, in particular, had been greatly weakened (e.g. France had been split between supporters of the pro-German Vichy regime and the Free French).

f) Italy was driven out of her colonies during the war: Ethiopia regained her independence and Libya and Somalia became United Nations responsibilities and moved rapidly towards independence.

The achievement of independence

Independence returned to Africa very quickly: in 1945 Egypt, Ethiopia and Liberia were the only independent African states (South Africa was independent under white minority rule); by 1978 Namibia was the only part of Africa still under colonial rule. Independence also came with slight preparation either poltically or economically.

In the late 1940s and early 1950s the more outspoken nationalist parties in many parts of Africa were suppressed and their leaders were imprisoned. The British were usually the first to realise that repression would not work. Kenya and Zimbabwe, settler strongholds, were the only parts of British Africa where serious violence broke out. From the late 1940s onwards the British territories moved rapidly towards independence. Indirect rule was replaced by elected local authorities and the legislative councils were expanded and given greater powers, and administrative experience was given to Africans. Eventually elections were held to much expanded legislative councils, and the executive councils were replaced by African ministers (internal self-government), a stage very quickly followed by full independence.

The French for long tried to divert nationalist demands for independence by promising varying forms of autonomy within a French community. France's defeat in Indo-China in 1954 and the outbreak of war in Algeria left France in a weak position to resist the movement towards independence throughout Africa. Most of French Africa became independent in 1960, often with little preparation and with great economic dependence on France. Belgium granted Zaïre independence with no preparation at all. Portugal was the only colonial power which completely refused to accept the rapid movement towards independence and fought guerrilla wars throughout the 1960s and early 1970s in all her territories in a futile attempt to retain control.

International opinion greatly encouraged African nationalism and weakened the determination of the colonial powers to retain control. The charter of the United Nations Organisation founded in 1949 emphasised the need for freedom, and at the United Nations the newly-independent Asian states urged the ending of colonialism in Africa. The first major conference of non-aligned nations held at Bandung in Indonesia in 1955 strongly criticised colonialism. General Nasser of Egypt did much to encourage and support nationalists throughout Africa, and Nkrumah, who led Ghana to independence in 1957, was an inspiration to nationalist politicians in the rest of Africa.

22

Post-independence Africa

During the last quarter of a century virtually the whole of Africa has gained its independence: in the twelve years 1957–69 forty-two countries achieved independence and there are now over fifty independent African nations. Probably the most important inheritance from the colonial period were the boundaries of the present states. Most of the modern boundaries date from the period of the partition, and most modern states are larger than pre-colonial political units. Despite the fact that many of the boundaries are illogical (e.g. the boundaries of The Gambia), very few boundary changes have occurred since independence. During the mid 1970s, however, boundary problems became more frequent and more serious (e.g. Somali claims to parts of Ethiopia and Kenya and rivalry between Morocco and Mauritania over the future of Western Sahara). The colonial boundaries inherited by the states of modern Africa have created serious problems for some of these states. Fourteen African states are completely land-locked (without access to the sea). Several other states are almost land-locked (e.g. Zaïre) and others are of very irregular shape (e.g. Zambia which is almost cut into two by Shaba province of Zaïre).

Virtually all of Africa has gained its independence, but serious problems remain. The liberation struggle in southern Africa continues: the African population of Namibia is now certain of majority rule, but doubt still remains about timing and methods. The vast economic and military strength of the minority white regime in South Africa remains a major obstacle to the full completion of liberation. In the rest of Africa independence has not always produced either the rapid social and economic development which was hoped for or political stability. Many independent states have remained closely tied to their former colonial ruler, thus preventing full political and economic independence. Most African states are very aware of the dangers of neo-colonialism (the continuation or revival of foreign interference in African affairs).

Despite the problems facing present-day Africa, there are many hopeful signs. Africa has great resources both natural and human. Rapid and impressive development has taken place since independence in some fields (e.g. in parts of the economy and in education). Over-generalisation must be avoided since Africa is so large and diverse.

Political development

Post-independence leaders

During the last years of colonial rule it became clear that the small educated elite, who led the nationalist parties and played an increasingly important role in the civil service and the professions, would take over full control of the government at independence. The leaders of Africa since independence have had varying success in the major task of nation-building. Some countries have been very much influenced by a single, outstanding political leader (e.g. Senghor, Kenyatta, Nyerere, Kaunda).

The new African leaders were left with serious, unresolved internal problems by the colonial powers. In particular, they have had to face problems of fostering national unity and encouraging economic growth. Many of the new leaders became unpopular for a variety of reasons.

a) Inheriting weak social and economic structures meant that progress did not take place as rapidly as the people had been led to expect during the struggle for independence.

b) The unequal colonial salary structure and the privileges and fringe benefits previously enjoyed by the colonial rulers were often preserved.

c) Various types of disunity (ethnic, regional, religious) had been minimised during the nationalist struggle for independence when all had united against the common enemy. Once independence had been achieved, these disunities reappeared.

d) There was also a lot of criticism of the very large spending which sometimes took place on prestige projects of little value to the masses (e.g. the very expensive complex built in Accra by Nkrumah for the 1965 OAU meeting).

This growing unpopularity made the post-independence rulers even more critical of and determined to suppress any opposition. Opposition political parties (often ethnic- or regionally-based) were often seen as a threat to national unity and a luxury that could not be afforded. To suppress opposition, methods used by the colonial authorities were continued and in some cases extended (e.g. strict censorship of the press, unacceptably wide government powers). Those in power tried to control all the institutions of the state; measures were taken to ensure support from such groups as trade unions and students unions, and powerful traditional rulers were not allowed to remain as rival centres of power (e.g. in Lesotho and Uganda). These conflicts between the ruling parties and any opposition often led to the destruction of the multi-party parliamentary systems inherited from the colonial period and to the establishment of either one-party states or military rule.

One-party states

Nkrumah and the Convention People's Party in Ghana led the way in the creation of a one-party state. From 1957 to 1960 Nkrumah did everything possible to consolidate and strengthen the position of himself and his party (e.g. CPP politicians were appointed as regional commissioners, anti-CPP chiefs were dismissed, and the regional opposition parties were persecuted). In 1960 Nkrumah introduced a new constitution creating a one-party state and giving himself increased powers. During the 1960s many others followed Ghana's example and became one-party states (e.g. Ivory Coast, Zambia and Tanzania).

Fear of disunity and the desire for rapid change help to explain the establishment of one-party states. Many have argued that a one-party state is more suited to traditional African social organisation and that it is necessary in order to foster national unity. Certainly a one-party state has the advantage of greater unity and continuity and avoids the danger of rival parties as a possible means for foreign interference. One of the most successful one-party states has been Tanzania under Nyerere whose programme of African Socialism ('Ujamaa') has done much to promote unity, equality, stability and development. Among possible disadvantages of a one-party system are the following: it may lead to an increase in inefficiency and corruption; it may lead to oppressive rule and less freedom; it may ignore minority groups; it is very difficult to change the government except by violent revolution.

Military rule

At independence, most countries had very small armies with no political role. The army played little part in the nationalist struggle for independence (except in Algeria, Zimbabwe and the Portuguese colonies, where independence was achieved only after a long military struggle). Within a decade of independence, however, military coups established military rule in almost half the nations of Africa. The first military regimes were established in North Africa in the 1950s (Egypt in 1952 and Sudan in 1958). Far more widespread were the military coups in the mid and late 1960s. Military rule was established in 1965 in Algeria, Zaïre and Benin; in 1966 in Upper Volta, Central African Republic, Nigeria, Ghana and Burundi; in 1967 in Sierra Leone and Togo, and in 1968 in the Congo Republic and Mali. Since the mid 1960s military coups have been less frequent, but military rule has been established in several more countries (e.g. Somalia, Libya, Ethiopia and Liberia). Several countries (e.g. Nigeria, Ghana, Sudan) have experienced more than one military coup, Benin having no less than five during the 1960s.

The causes for the establishment of military rule vary from country to country, but certain common factors can be distinguished.
a) The post-independence leaders lacking the means to achieve their independence promises, soon became unpopular.
b) In many countries the political party in power strengthened its position to such an extent that only the military had the strength to overthrow it.
c) Corruption, waste and the failure to achieve rapid economic progress caused much disillusionment.
d) Political parties became increasingly repressive in their attempts to retain power, thus producing increasing political violence, so that only the army could maintain order.
e) Ethnic and regional rivalries and tensions often played a part in producing military coups.
f) In some countries rivalries between the younger officers and the more senior officers was a crucial factor.
Almost everywhere the civilian governments overthrown by military coups were unpopular and ineffective and so military rule, which promised to end corruption and disunity, was at first welcomed. Most military rulers promised to hand back to civilian government in the near future, but this has proved difficult and has only taken place in a few countries (e.g. Ghana and Nigeria). Military

governments have often failed to produce the social and economic reforms promised and this has then made them unpopular (e.g. the third military coup in Nigeria in 1975). Military rule has similar advantages to a one-party system (especially in promoting unity), but there are also possible disadvantages (e.g. it may lead to oppressive rule and it may produce an uneconomically large army).

Disunity

One of the greatest problems facing independent African states has been disunity arising from ethnic rivalry, as ethnic feelings often appear to be stronger than nationalism. This has not been a great problem in North Africa, in most parts of which nation-states had developed before colonial rule. In the rest of Africa, however, most countries contain a large number of different ethnic groups (e.g. about 120 in Tanzania and even more in Zaïre and Nigeria). The period of colonial rule did little to promote national unity and political experience in the business of government. The nationalist parties which led the way to independence were often regional in origin (e.g. in Zaïre). Since independence ethnic rivalries have not only produced considerable tension, but in several cases have led to full-scale wars (e.g. in Zaïre, where several secession movements – the most serious of which was that in Shaba province – produced anarchy in the early 1960s; in Nigeria where the south-east tried to seceed – the Biafra War; in Sudan; in Chad; and in Ethiopia).

Several factors help to explain the prevalence of internal disunity and instability.

a) The countries of modern Africa are new and were given little chance to develop unity during the colonial divide and rule period.

b) Since independence there has been much ethnic and regional competition for jobs and amenities.

c) In some countries where one ethnic group is much larger or more educated than the others there has been the fear of domination by one group.

d) In some cases an ethnic group split between two countries (e.g. the Ewe split between Ghana and Togo) have struggled to unite themselves in one country.

Nigeria has attempted to ease ethnic tension by a federal constitution and the creation of more states. Most countries, however, have turned towards strong, centralised, unitary, one-party governments in an attempt to promote greater unity. It is too soon to judge the degree of success achieved in strengthening unity, but attempted secession and civil wars must be regarded as extreme cases: the growth of the economy and of education has in many countries helped to strengthen national unity.

Economic development

Most African countries have remained economically weak with a low standard of living and a continual struggle against poverty (eighteen out of the twenty-nine United Nations least-developed countries are in Africa). The failure to produce rapid economic development has led to great dissatisfaction and has been the cause of much political instability. Some countries (e.g. Ivory Coast) have developed along capitalist lines (economic development largely in the hands of private investors and businessmen), while others (e.g. Tanzania) have moved towards socialism (greater government control and stimulation of the economy) – in fact Nyerere in Tanzania has developed a distinctive philosophy of African Socialism.

Difficulties preventing rapid economic growth

a) Colonial rule left most of Africa with serious economic problems.
- During the colonial period many areas became totally dependent on the export of a single cash crop or mineral (e.g. cocoa in Ghana and copper in Zambia).
- There was very little industrial development during the colonial period.
- Foreign trade was monopolised by large European trading companies.
- There was little trade between different African territories.
- Communications were developed only for external trade, not for internal or inter-territorial trade.
- The trade of most countries was almost completely with their colonial ruler.
b) Lack of skilled manpower and capital has made industrialisation difficult and African countries have found it very difficult to compete with the major industrial nations of the world.
c) Most of Africa has a low density of population which has meant a small domestic market and a shortage of labour. Rapid population growth has limited the effects of economic development.
d) Much of Africa has insufficient rainfall and poor soil.
e) Many of the economically-weak African countries have failed to free themselves from the close economic links with their former colonial ruler.

Achievements

The difficulties just mentioned are serious, but it must be remembered that much of Africa has great economic resources, especially minerals and hydro-electricity. Impressive achievements in many areas of the economy have been made since independence.

a) There has been a much increased government expenditure on education, and educational facilities have expanded considerably (e.g. the number of universities in black Africa increased from five to twenty-eight between 1946 and 1965, and since then the number has more than doubled). Both Nigeria and Kenya have introduced universal, free primary education.
b) Many countries have begun to industrialise as rapidly as possible and are now not only self-sufficient in many manufactured goods but even export some.
c) Power supplies have increased greatly largely through hydro-electric schemes (e.g. the Aswan, Kainji and Volta dams).
d) Mineral production has increased and new mineral reserves have been discovered and developed (e.g. oil in Libya, Gabon and Nigeria). By 1979 the value of Nigerian oil revenues amounted to ₦9·0 billion a year and contributed some 90 per cent of the total revenues.)

e) There has been a great improvement in communications, especially in the building of roads and the development of air transport.

f) African participation in and control of all aspects of the economy has greatly increased.

g) Agricultural development has been less rapid than was hoped, but many governments have done much to improve agricultural output by encouraging mechanisation, irrigation and the use of fertilisers.

h) Most countries have succeeded in diversifying their economies and gradual progress has been made in improving standards of living.

Pan-Africanism and religious cooperation

Pan-Africanism

Pan-African feeling (the desire for a united Africa) has developed out of an awareness of African cultural unity, a desire to present a united African front in world affairs and a wish to assist those still struggling for freedom from colonial rule. Pan-African ideas began in the late nineteenth and early twentieth centuries both in Africa and among black people in America. Several pan-African congresses were held between 1919 and 1945; the early congresses were moderate and mostly run by black Americans, but the last of these congresses held in Manchester in 1945 was more African-orientated (Nkrumah and Kenyatta were among the Africans who attended) and more radical, and called for an eventual union of independent African states.

In the late 1950s and early 1960s pan-Africanism became very important, largely thanks to Nkrumah. Pan-Africanism became more practical and more purely African but individual nationalism remained stronger than pan-Africanism and many mistrusted Nkrumah's ambitions to lead a united Africa. Pan-African feeling culminated in the formation of the Organisation of African Unity (OAU) in 1963, after a series of All-African Peoples' Congresses which started with one in Accra in 1958. The OAU, which comprises an assembly of heads of state, a council of ministers, several specialised commissions and a permanent secretariat, fell far short of Nkrumah's hopes of a fully-united Africa, but it has survived and has achieved much.

a) Some achievements of the OAU are as follows.

- It has supported liberation movements, helped to remove colonialism from the rest of Africa and guarded against neo-colonialism.

- It has served as a stabilising force, trying to mediate and encourage peace in serious crises (e.g. during the Biafra War).

- It has helped to prevent war by settling minor border disputes.

- It has provided regular contact between heads of state which has encouraged more inter-state cooperation.

- It has presented a united African voice on world issues.

b) Several weaknesses have prevented the OAU from achieving more.

- Individual nationalism has remained stronger than pan-Africanism, and all states have been unwilling to surrender real power.

- There have been serious differences of approach to world and African issues. In the early and mid 1960s a moderate and a radical group emerged: the

Monrovia group (including such countries as Liberia, Nigeria and Sudan) was conservative and pro-Western, while the Casablanca group (including such countries as Ghana, Guinea and Algeria) was more radical and pro-communist. At the 1964 OAU meeting at Cairo this division showed itself in the form of pro- and anti-Nkrumah groups, and seven ex-French territories refused to attend the 1965 meeting.

- There were also differences in language and approach inherited from the colonial period (e.g. the ex-French territories have retained close links in such organisations as OCAM).
- The OAU has been hindered by lack of funds.
- There have been serious disputes between members (e.g. between Somalia and Kenya and Somalia and Ethiopia).
- After military coups many countries have focused their attention more on internal problems than on wider African affairs.

Regional cooperation

The small population, awkward shape and weakness of most African states has encouraged various forms of regional cooperation. Many difficulties stand in the way of effective regional cooperation, such as inequalities in the size, population and development of countries, poor communications, and differences in religion, language and environment. Attempts at full political union (e.g. the Mali Federation, the Ghana-Guinea Union) have failed, but, despite the problems, there has been some success in economic cooperation and in more specific, localised inter-state projects.

The following are examples of large-scale regional cooperation.

a) The East African Community formed in 1967 achieved much in its first years, although recently it has broken down.
b) The former French territories have formed several organisations beginning with the Brazzaville group in 1960 and culminating in the *Organisation Commune Africain et Malagashe* (OCAM) in 1965.
c) In 1975 the Economic Council of West African States (ECOWAS) was formed.

The following are examples of more specific inter-state cooperation.

a) The Mano River Union between Sierra Leone and Liberia.
b) Inter-state cooperation in the development of communications (e.g. the Lagos to Mombasa road).
c) The customs union (UDEAC) between the former French states of west-central Africa.

Independent Africa and the world

Since independence, Africa has played an important role in world affairs. Several factors help to explain the considerable world interest in Africa.

a) By 1970, one-third of the member-states of the United Nations were African.
b) Africa is important to the rest of the world economically, especially as a producer of valuable minerals.
c) Many parts of Africa are important in world strategy, and the great world

powers (the USSR and the USA) have both tried to extend their rivalry to Africa (e.g. recent conflicts in the north-east corner of Africa).

Different African countries have, of course, pursued different foreign policies, but certain common elements can be distinguished.

a) Foreign policy has changed frequently, as individual leaders have exerted great influence.

b) Similar objectives have been pursued: peace, economic prosperity, the ending of colonial rule and apartheid in southern Africa.

c) African countries are not aligned with either of the main power blocs (the USSR and the USA).

Militarily and economically Africa is weak, and most countries have therefore found full political and economic non-alignment difficult to achieve. Economically many have remained closely tied to their former colonial ruler (e.g. at the Yaoundé Convention in 1963 eighteen African states established reciprocal trade preferences with the European Economic Community) and politically many have remained members of such organisations as the British Commonwealth and the French Community. Most have managed to prevent foreign aid leading to political dependence, but even in the early 1980s, non-African military activity can be found in many parts of Africa.

It is, however, important to remember that underdevelopment and instability are not inevitable: Africa possesses great human and natural resources. In the 1960s Africa was annually producing ninety-eight per cent of the world's diamonds, sixty-five per cent of the world's palm-oil, sixty per cent of the world's cocoa and fifty per cent of the world's gold, and very valuable oil and uranium deposits have also been discovered in several countries. Not all African countries have suffered from political instability, and several countries have made impressive recoveries from serious crises.

Very great progress has been made since independence, and it is to be hoped that progress will continue and that Africa in the 1980s will play an increasingly important role in world affairs.